STORY-LIVES OF MASTER ARTISTS

STORY-LIVES OF MASTER ARTISTS

1953 Revision

BY ANNA CURTIS CHANDLER

With Twenty-three Reproductions from Paintings

J. B. Lippincott Company
PHILADELPHIA
AND NEW YORK

PRINTED IN THE UNITED STATES OF AMERICA

Library of Congress Catalog Card Number 53-5426

DEDICATED TO

The Girls and Boys
of
Hunter College Elementary School
New York City

Acknowledgments

The author is indebted to the late Henry W. Kent, formerly Secretary of the Metropolitan Museum of Art; to Professor Philip R. V. Curoe, Chairman of the Department of Education of Hunter College of the City of New York, and to Dr. Florence N. Brumbaugh, Principal of the Hunter College Elementary School who had the vision to sponsor weekly Audio-Visual Enrichment Programs. She thanks also the teachers and parents of the school for their interest and cooperation.

Grateful acknowledgment is made to the late Helen Dean Fish, for her invaluable guidance as children's book editor on both original series of STORY-LIVES OF MASTER ARTISTS and on this new edition.

Acknowledgment is made to *All Arts Magazine*, in which the story of Fra Filippo Lippi appeared, and to *St. Nicholas* magazine, in which the story of Winslow Homer was published.

INTRODUCTION

Because all children enjoy stories and because the lives of great personalities, dramatically told, stimulate ideals and often are an incentive for emulation, we have encouraged at Hunter College Elementary School weekly programs under such themes as "Courage," "In Spite of Handicaps," and "How the World of Yesterday Helps the U.S.A. Make a Better World for Tomorrow." The theme for the coming school year will be "They Who Serve Their Fellowmen."

Many of the personalities presented in these programs have been artists who, with their creative genius, are often in advance of their time and truly "serve their fellowmen" through works of art.

Anna Curtis Chandler has been called an "artist story teller," and is well fitted for her work through training and experience. Her dramatic audio-visual programs in the Metropolitan Museum of Art, New York City, were attended each week by thousands of girls and boys from the New York public schools. At Hunter she continues to write weekly story-programs, about great artists selected with the cooperation of our staff and the children of our school. She presents these story-lives to all the children. The programs are enriched by various audio-visual aids and integrate with many areas of the curriculum, following the yearly theme.

Students from the Department of Education in the college observe this vivid method of teaching, which is especially important for the children of the Hunter College Elementary School, many of whom will be leaders of tomorrow. Their enthusiastic response to this cultural stimulus is evidence of its value.

May this new edition of STORY-LIVES OF MASTER ARTISTS, with the author's dramatic portrayal of people and events inspire many girls and boys to further appreciation, study and practice of art.

Florence Brumbaugh
Principal, Hunter College Elementary School

AUTHOR'S FOREWORD

In these stories I have tried to make great artists seem real and human; the time in which they lived vivid; and their works treasures to be sought and enjoyed. They are true to the times in which the artists lived and to the facts of their lives, though sometimes I have added fancy to fact, always careful to make the fancy in keeping with the fact. As Mark Twain once said, "It might have happened; it may not have happened; but it *could* have happened."

I hope these story-lives may be steppingstones to the enjoyment of the work of these and other artists in our own land and in lands across the sea; and that these lives of high endeavor and accomplishment may serve as inspiration to future artists and beauty lovers.

Before each story is a brief descriptive account of the artist's time, a biographical summary to supplement the story and a short list of some of his works which will be of interest to boys and girls.

Once interest is created through the story, every boy and girl will, I hope, want to find in the library books which will tell more about the wonderful works these artists have created. Perhaps some will be ambitious enough to make a collection of photographs, postcards, and miniature color-prints of great works of art, and best of all, some day, visit art galleries to see some of the original paintings.

Just as in my Story Programs given to thousands of boys and girls in the Metropolitan Museum of Art, and in Audio-Visual Enrichment Programs for the children at Hunter College Elementary School, and the college students who come to "observe," I try to make great personalities live, the historic backgrounds vivid, and their lives an incentive to boys and girls who will, many of them, be the leaders of tomorrow. The lives of master artists, and their contribution of beauty will serve as inspiration to many who may become our future artists, or patrons of art. For this new volume of story-lives of master artists, I have selected from both series, those artists who have been the favorites with girls and boys.

Art, like music, is a common language, understood by all people in all lands. May these stories, woven around artists and their times, help in its understanding, and may they lead to a greater enjoyment of beauty, wherever it is discovered. An artist of Italy once said, "If you get simple Beauty and naught else, you get about the best thing God invented."

Anna Curtis Chandler

January, 1953

CONTENTS

PAGE

GIOTTO:
The Painter Who Saw and Thought for Himself 1

FILIPPO LIPPI:
A Boy of Old Florence 15

LEONARDO DA VINCI:
The Magician Painter 27

ALBRECHT DÜRER:
Maximilian's Favorite Painter 41

MICHELANGELO
Of the Gigantic Picture Book 54

RAPHAEL:
A Boy Artist of Urbino 67

EL GRECO:
Painter of Spain 80

PETER PAUL RUBENS:
A Page Who Became a Painter 89

FRANS HALS:
A Jolly Dutchman Who Painted Pictures 98

ANTHONY VAN DYCK:
Court Painter to King Charles the First 110

DIEGO VELAZQUEZ:
At the Court of a King Who Seldom Smiled 122

REMBRANDT:
Master of Light and Shadow 135

JOHANNES VERMEER:
Through Sunny Dutch Windows 149

PAGE

THOMAS GAINSBOROUGH and JOSHUA REYNOLDS:
Two Painters Who Loved Children 163

GILBERT STUART:
The Painter of Our First President 177

JEAN BAPTISTE COROT:
A Painter of Springtime 187

JEAN FRANÇOIS MILLET:
Who Believed in Beauty in Everyday Work 199

JAMES MCNEILL WHISTLER:
An Artist Who Made His Mother Famous 212

WINSLOW HOMER:
The Song of the Sea 223

EDWIN AUSTIN ABBEY:
The Artist Who Pictured King Arthur's Court 238

Bibliography 251

Illustrations

(in this order following page 144)

St. Francis Preaching to the Birds . . . . *Giotto*
Madonna, Child and Two Angels . *Fra Filippo Lippi*
The Madonna of the Rocks . . *Leonardo da Vinci*
Portrait of Himself . . . . . . *Albrecht Dürer*
The Creation of Adam . . . . . *Michelangelo*
Statue of David . . . . *Michelangelo*
Madonna, Child, and Little Saint John ("Madonna of the Chair") . . . . *Raphael*
St. George and the Dragon . . . . . *Raphael*
View of Toledo . . . . *El Greco*
Rubens' Two Sons, Albert and Nicolas . . . . *Peter Paul Rubens*
The Musician . . . . *Franz Hals*
Children of Charles I . . . . *Anthony Van Dyck*
The Maids of Honor . . . . *Velazquez*
The Night Watch, or The Company of Captain Frans Banning Cocq . . . *Rembrandt van Ryn*
Young Girl with a Water Jug . . . *Johannes Vermeer*
Georgiana Augusta Frederica Seymour . . . . *Sir Joshua Reynolds*
The Blue Boy . . . . . . *Thomas Gainsborough*
George Washington . . . . *Gilbert Stuart*
A Path Through the Trees . . . . . . *Corot*
The Gleaners . . . . *Jean François Millet*

Fog Warning . . . . *Winslow Homer*
Portrait of the Artist's Mother; Arrangement in Grey and Black . . . . . *James McNeill Whistler*
Galahad the Deliverer . . . . . *Edwin Austin Abbey*

STORY-LIVES OF MASTER ARTISTS

GIOTTO

1266–1337

BEFORE THE STORY

GIOTTO DI BONDONE, usually called Giotto, was born over six centuries ago in an Italian hill village near Florence, in the district of Vespignano. He spent his life beautifying with architecture, sculpture and painting, various Italian cities, including Assisi, Florence, Rome, Naples and Padua.

It is with Florence that Giotto is chiefly identified, for in that city he designed the slender, graceful bell tower, often called Giotto's Tower. With another sculptor, Andrea Pisano, he decorated it with carved pictures of people going about their everyday work, a thing no painter had dared to do before.

Before he designed this "campanile" or bell tower, however, Giotto had painted many pictures for churches. In this long-ago time, when there were no printed books and no illustrations such as we have today, these paintings took their place, and taught the lessons of the church. Before Giotto, the church decided upon the rules artists must follow in making their religious pictures. The colors were very lovely, glowing almost like jewels, the gold sky decorative, the line and pattern beautiful. But the figures were flat and lifeless.

Giotto had the courage to depart from the formal, set

rules prescribed for painters, believing that pictures with natural scenes and real-looking people were just as much to the glory of God. In this way he was a leader in the making of more real-looking pictures, studying the scenes and people he saw, making the sky blue, the hills and trees as he saw them, the Holy Mother like a real mother, the Holy Child like a real baby, and the Wise Men like Florentine nobles. Every line in his drapery suggests the form beneath.

Giotto expressed the time in which he lived, a time when people were beginning to be curious about the world in which they lived, about scientific laws, religion, the learning of the Greeks and the Romans, reviving the love of beauty for its own sake.

It was a time of individual thought, and Giotto was one of the pioneers, believing with the good Saint Francis of Assisi whom he pictured talking to the birds, that religion belongs to everyday life. Giotto led the way for the great artists of Italy who came after him.

Some of Giotto's Paintings:

SCENES FROM THE LIFE OF CHRIST AND THE VIRGIN (*frescos*)
Arena Chapel, Padua

SCENES FROM THE LIFE OF SAINT FRANCIS (*frescos*)
Church of Santa Croce, Florence

SCENES FROM THE LIFE OF SAINT JOHN EVANGELIST (*frescos*)
Church of Santa Croce, Florence

SCENES FROM THE LIFE OF SAINT FRANCIS (*by Giotto and a pupil*)
Church of Saint Francis, Assisi

GIOTTO, THE PAINTER WHO SAW AND THOUGHT FOR HIMSELF

There was wonderment in the little village of Colle, up among the hills, not many miles from the famous and beautiful city of Florence in Italy. It was over two hundred years earlier than the memorable year when a man of Italy, Cristofero Colombo, started out from a Spanish harbor to sail across an unknown sea in order to find land to the westward. Rumor had it that young Giotto di Bondone was going to Florence to learn to paint!

High around the little village towered the protecting Apennines, stretching up as if they longed to meet the soft blue of the spring sky, and producing upon their sloping sides the tender pasture land where the sheep liked so well to feed. Way down the hillsides wound the road which led to Florence with its palaces, its shops, its bridges crossing the river Arno, its learned men.

"Come within!" called Francesco Bondone, welcoming to his little home on the hillside some of the village folk who had arrived in person to see whether the rumor was true. "Sit thou here, Giovanni; and thou there, Antonio, on that bench yonder. Do thou, Giotto, place stools for Niccolo and his good wife. Aye, now that we are seated in comfort and can look out through the doorway towards our mountains covered with the purple of evening, ye shall hear of what happened this afternoon. Giotto shall begin until he comes to my part of the happening. Who says that one must live in the city below us to have strange things happen? Adventure came seeking us out today. Begin, my son!"

Giotto's brown eyes were dancing with excitement. He

looked happily and lovingly at his father, who had helped make his heart's desire come true that afternoon. He looked into the browned faces of the village folk, each one interested in and glad of his good fortune. He smiled into the wide and almost worshiping eyes of the boys who with him had so often tended sheep up on the hillsides.

"I am just the same, Luca, Benedetto—each and every one of you! I am not changed because my wish of going to Florence to study with the great painter is coming true. I am thy playmate and companion still, just the shepherd boy of Vespignano, Giotto di Bondone."

"Tell us!" begged the boys, almost consumed with curiosity to hear from Giotto himself just what had happened. "Nay, keep us waiting no longer, thou unfeeling boy," begged Giovanni and the others from the village. "We all are impatient to hear!"

Giotto clasped his brown knees with his still browner hands. Little stars seemed to shine from the depths of his eyes as he talked. "Thou wilt remember, Luca, Benedetto, that I left you on the hillside today and went down on the slope where I had seen such green grass that I knew the sheep would like to feed upon it, and where mine eyes had caught sight of golden yellow flowers beneath the apple trees. Always am I seeking for new flowers and birds as thou dost well know, Benedetto, for thine eyes have helped me hunt and watched my fingers try to picture them."

"Even so, Giotto," affirmed Benedetto. "Always thou art drawing when thou art not busy keeping thy sheep from straying into some lonely pass or thicket. There is scarcely a smooth rock near the pasture land which has not some picture scratched upon it!"

Giotto laughed. "Poor Benedetto! my picturemaking has often tried thee sore when thou didst wish to play a game! Hear, now, what happened on this very day. 'Tis almost like the wonderful stories which the good friar tells us.

"I was lying on the sweet grass beneath an olive tree, watching the sheep nibbling greedily upon the tender grass, and fondling the lamb which strayed away the other day and hurt its foot; listening to the wind music playing among the silver leaves over my head, and thinking of my dream, my wish. Thou dost know, Benedetto, and thou, too, Luca, that one day I might go to the city of Florence, a-traveling along yonder road which goes winding in the midst of the green, less and less wide till it becomes a slender ribbon ending in that city where men do great things, build great palaces, carve great statues, paint pictures for the holy church, write wise words and music-making verses, and play upon the lyre and the harp before great men.

"All within me began to yearn, good friends, till I sprang upright and some voice whispered, 'Come, shepherd boy, come to Florence that there thy fingers may learn the way to paint!' There was still one smooth-surfaced rock nearby, not far from the road which wound its way over the hills and down to the wider one which led to the city. That rock I had not covered with pictures of clouds, or flowers, or graceful bending trees; so quickly I chipped a piece from the side and with the sharp edge I began to draw. And what dost thou think I chose this time? *Bene!* Luca, thou hast guessed it; my little lamb lying there upon the soft, warm grass, lazily nibbling at it. My piece of stone was just sharp enough, the rock so wide and smooth. Never had mine eyes seen so clearly or my fingers moved so surely, and my lamb kept quite still, just once or twice gazing at me with a puzzled look, to know what I might be doing.

" 'Ah!' I cried, at last; 'thou art finished, lamb!' and heard a strange noise by my side. There, coming to me from the road that wound its way from Florence, was a man, a stranger to these hills as I could well see by his dress and manner. Waiting for him on horseback on the winding road were his companions, and from their velvet cloaks and plumed hats, I well knew they were city folk.

" 'A good day and a happy one,' said the tall stranger smiling down upon me in a kindly way. 'Thou art a maker of pictures, my eyes tell me. Yonder drowsy white-fleeced lamb would, methinks, own the picture of him on thy flat rock as a good likeness. I saw thy fingers busy at thy picturemaking as I journeyed with my good friends yonder over the long road to the City of Flowers after going to plan for the painting of a Holy Mother and Babe for a church in a village not far from here. Is there a painter here among the hilltops who has taught thee?'

"How I laughed, Benedetto, for as thou dost know I taught myself by patient practice day after day, and so I told him. 'Art thou going to the city of Florence yonder?' I asked him, glancing at the far view of that city, like a dream city, as it nestles among the blue-veiled hills. He nodded, smiling. 'Perchance, Sire,' I asked him, breathless, 'wilt thou see the great painter whose fame has come to Vespignano and even here upon the hillsides, Cimabue, whose picture of the Holy Mother for one of the churches in yonder city is so lovely that 'twas borne in procession through the streets of Florence that it might be viewed by the many who thronged to see it?'

"The stranger's smile deepened; he swept his broad hat from his head and bowed before me—"

"He was the great Cimabue himself!" guessed Benedetto, jumping up to grasp his work- and playfellow, Giotto, by the hand. "It is a marvel," breathed the simple shepherd folk, like the boys and girls quite ready for a miracle to happen. "Thy heart's desire was granted in God," murmured the old grandfather from his armchair in the chimney corner. "Our Giotto will be journeying to the big city of Florence!" sang the dark-eyed boys and girls, quite without envy. Giotto's father said never a word but rested his hand upon his son's shoulder.

"Thou didst guess right, Benedetto," Giotto went on; "the stranger was the great Cimabue renowned in Florence and everywhere roundabout; he who painted the great altarpiece and whose skilful fingers can form pictures patterned from little cubes of glass and stone, called mosaic work. This is what he then said to me: 'If thou canst thus picture thy pet lamb on a smooth rock for paper or canvas, with a sharp stone in place of pencil or brush, thou canst do great things with the proper tools and with the training such as I can give thee. Come with me to the city yonder that I may teach thee!' "

"Thou wilt see grand palaces and high towers instead of our little cottages," murmured starry-eyed Angelica. "Great ladies and princes gay in fine clothes, grand processions all gay with bright colors!"

"Not unless my father is willing," answered Giotto gravely, looking up into his father's eyes, his own full of affection.

"It is my turn to tell the story now," his father said slowly, holding him close. "The painter from the great city came to me with my boy. 'Canst spare thy shepherd lad?' he asked me courteously, 'that I may take him to the city of Florence and teach him in my workshop? I will take good care of him, Francesco Bondone, and one day he will give great honor to thy name, for his fingers, his mind, and his eyes need but good training to enable him to paint beautiful pictures for our churches, that folk may go to enjoy them every day.' "

"So thou didst tell the fine stranger that our lad could go with him in his care," said Grandfather in the chimney corner. "I heard thee, Francesco. We shall miss him here, but we shall be proud of him, for the great painter will teach him the skill of his brush, the beauty of his color patterns."

"Come back to us soon, Giotto di Bondone!" called all the shepherd folk and those from Vespignano who had gathered to watch him start off for Florence in company with the painter and his companions.

Giotto sat upon his richly harnessed horse and looked back upon his home so secure amidst the trees and sheltered by the high surrounding hills. He gazed long upon the mountainsides, yellow, green, gray; upon the carpets of bright flowers, the yellow streams and those like silver dashing down the mountainsides; the snowy sheep, and last of all his family and friends. Now that his wish was coming true, now that he was really going to the great city he had so longed to see, he was loth to go.

"Fare ye well, Father, Grandfather, Benedetto—all of you! I won't forget and I'll come back to you!"

The plumes on the horses' heads trembled, the gold, the silver, the jewels gleamed, light and shadow played upon the velvets and made gay and bright the scarlet cloth, as the procession started. Banners waved, trumpets set the hillsides and mountaintops to echoing, as did the farewell greetings.

"Do not forget us, Giotto! Come back to thy family and

thy friends who love thee. Do not forget us, for we shall be thinking of thee and thy success will make us proud!"

Sometimes Giotto thought, as he worked hard day after day in the master's workshop in the heart of the great city of Florence which was in the hills he had so longed to visit, that he wanted to go back to tending his sheep out beneath the sunny, blue sky and amidst the velvet soft grass. Then he would shake his head as if he would shake the longing from his mind, and work harder than before.

"My pictures are going to look like the real, everyday people I see around me," he would promise himself; "not stiff, like the pictures painted according to a pattern for the church. The Holy Mother shall look like the real mother, so gentle, so beautiful, so tender, who takes her *bambino* each sunny day to the piazza near the cathedral in order that he may feed the birds. The babe shall look like him. One day I shall make a picture of the good saint of Assisi, who only a few score years ago went among the people teaching them to be kind and good and helpful to one another, pure in heart, humble in mind, and filled with love for all people. I shall picture him with the birds flying around him for he understood them so well and loved them so much that they could talk together. The birds shall be like the real birds that I have seen so many times flying across the blue sea of the sky as I tended the sheep upon the hillside, and the trees, like the people and animals, shall seem to have form as in life. Thus shall the people who go daily to the churches to enjoy their holy pictures see the beauty of Nature, of form, of color, instead of just set patterns. Surely, there can be no harm in painting beautiful pictures, for beauty as seen through the eyes and heard through the ears gives so much happiness.

Giotto did bring honor to his family and friends in the little hillside village. And Giotto did give happiness and refreshment to many people through his pictures, which were quite different from those painted before. All the old stiffness was gone, and although they may look strange to us compared with later pictures, yet they were the beginning of beautiful pictures, and paved the way for more natural and beautiful ones.

Of course Giotto did not become a great painter all at once! There was a great deal to learn first; how to make purposeful, beautiful lines, how to use his brush and put on the pure colors so that they would make a pleasing color pattern. Long he watched his master at work before he was allowed to paint pictures of his own. It is said that one day Cimabue left Giotto alone at his task. Giotto, who still was a boy filled with the love of fun and of pranks, thought that he would play a joke upon the master. He painted a fly right on the tip of the nose of a figure Cimabue was painting! Then he watched to see what the master would do. Impatiently upon his return, Cimabue strode up to the picture and tried to brush off that very real-looking fly! How could he scold his pupil when he had proved himself so very apt and had turned out to be such a fine painter? How the shepherd boys on the hillside—Benedetto and Luca—and even his father, and his grandfather in the chimney corner must have chuckled when they heard about it!

Giotto greatly beautified that city of Florence to which he had so longed to go when he was a shepherd boy. The people of Florence loved beauty so much that they felt they must have it all around them—beautiful paintings, carvings, buildings. So, you see, the artists of Florence had many requests for their work. There was a religious reason, too, for they wanted to do their saints honor by having pictures of their lives and miracles pictured upon some chapel wall. Also, these pictures served the everyday folk as great religious picture books. Besides these reasons, Florence wanted to have better pictures and sculpture and architecture than any other city of Italy! There were guilds, or societies for members of the various crafts—goldsmiths, weavers, sculptors, painters, druggists (who, by the way, made the color for the painters), and many other societies of good workmen. The painter was considered a fine craftsman, and had a studio or workshop called a *bottega,* where he carried out the orders which he received. In the workshop were assistants and apprentices who were learning the trade or art. A painter of Florence had to know many things, how to grind his colors, paint upon walls of churches, how to gild (for often painters made pictures upon the front of marriage chests), how to paint upon wooden panels.

For painting upon church walls, he must be able to work boldly and quickly, for the part of a plaster wall planned for a day's work was covered with a new coat, and the colors used went down deep into the wet plaster, uniting with it. Just think! a wrong or uncertain brush stroke meant scraping off all the wet plaster, and starting over again! For painting upon a wooden panel, a great deal of patience was required, and very careful, delicate work. The wooden panel was covered with layers of the very finest plaster of Paris in glue and rubbed and polished until it was very smooth. Then the design was copied upon it very, very carefully, and if there was to be a gold background as there so often was in the early days, it was applied in pure gold leaf. The paints, mixed with egg, were thick and had to be applied very slowly. The colors were so glowing and sparkling, however, that they quite made up for the painstaking work. Giotto was a master of this difficult craft.

Not only did Giotto paint, but he carved and builded. Up towards the sunny sky rose the tall Bell Tower close to the great cathedral. Like a fair, white lily it still soars lightly upward, catching the sunlight and colors, and carved upon it are marble pictures, some from his own hand, some from the hands of other artists who like him were glad to break away from the old stiffness and think for themselves. In one of these pictures a shepherd peers from the opening of his tent, watching the sheep, just as Giotto and the other boys used to watch the sheep on the hillside. No doubt the sheep were pictures of some he had watched so carefully each day. By the side of the tent he carved a jolly, lifelike little dog.

"How wonderful is this Giotto who came to us from near Vespignano," we can hear the folk of Florence say. "He will beautify our churches so that we shall enjoy the holy pictures more and more. So plump and soft the Holy Child looks, so human the Holy Mother, like the mothers of Florence and their bambinos. Behold! we shall worship more earnestly than ever before, for the colors fairly seem to sing a song of praise!"

The people of many other towns and cities in Italy wanted his beautiful pictures, too. They wanted the walls of their churches made beautiful with his pictures told in color which gave their religious message to the people. Great men welcomed him; the famous poet Dante—who, just as Saint Francis of Assisi in his preaching, just as Giotto in his painting, tried to show in his verses a freedom of thought and good, simple teachings which all people could understand—had his likeness painted by him.

Even the Pope heard of him. He wanted the finest

painter to decorate the walls of the church of Saint Peter's in Rome. "Find him for me," he commanded. From one town to another his messengers went, asking each artist to give one of his paintings to show the Pope. Each gave his best, for each wanted the honor of working for the Pope and decorating that greatest of churches in Rome. When they reached Giotto, 'tis said he merely dipped his brush in red, rested his elbow on his side, and by a clever turn of his hand drew a perfect circle. "A strange picture to send His Holiness, the Pope," grumbled the messengers, looking contemptuously at a painter who was so simple as to send only a round O to the great Pope in Rome. Imagine their surprise when the Pope and the other wise men of that great city, decided that Giotto was just the painter they wanted to decorate the cathedral walls because he had made such a perfect circle unaided by a compass. "If he can make such a perfect O so freely with his fingers, those same fingers can make perfect pictures which will do honor to our Imperial City!" they said among themselves.

But I am sure that best of all you will like his pictures about the good Saint Francis, who taught people that religion meant doing good every day. Many of the pictures were painted upon the walls of the good saint's church in Assisi, a beautiful village not very far from Florence. He told all about the saint who chose to give up riches and go around preaching good, pure, and happy living to all God's creatures, even the birds.

Perhaps that was the story Giotto liked the best to paint, because it made him remember the way he had liked to watch the birds in flight when he was a boy. So he let his memory and his fancy go, and showed Saint Francis stretching out his hands as he talked with the birds who came fluttering to greet him:

"Be Thou praised, my Lord, with all Thy creatures, above all, Brother Sun,
Who gives the day and lightens us therewith.

. . . . . .

Be Thou praised, my Lord, of Sister Moon and the stars, in the Heaven hast Thou formed them, clear and precious and comely.
Be Thou praised, my Lord, of Brother Wind, and of the air, and the cloud, and of fair and all weather, by the which Thou givest to Thy creatures sustenance." *

Thus spoke the good Saint Francis, and he passed in and out among the birds and caressed them, saying to them, "My brothers the birds, much ought ye to praise your Creator, who hath clothed you with feathers and given you wings to fly, and hath made over unto you the pure air, and careth for you without your taking thought for yourselves." †

And straightway the birds lifted up their little heads and sang praises to the saint who had been rich but who gave up his wealth to the poor and who was humble enough to stop to talk with them. All of this Giotto understood, for though he was sought for by the great rulers to help beautify their cities, yet he, too, was humble enough to remember the birds, the sheep, the everyday folk, and to make pictures of them. So simple, so vivid was the way he told his picture stories in lines full of meaning, in pure, harmonious colors, that they filled the hearts of all with happiness and led the way to more real and beautiful pictures.

* *From the "Mirror of Perfection," translated by Robert Steele, based on documents and memoirs left by Friar Leo, and completed about 1318. See Everyman's Library.*

† *From the "Life of Saint Francis," by St. Bonaventura, 1260; translated by Miss E. Gurney Salter.*

FILIPPO LIPPI

1412(?)–1469

BEFORE THE STORY

Filippo Lippi lived in Florence during a very wonderful age. It was the age of discovery, not only for those who, like Columbus, went sailing over strange waters to new lands, but in Science and Art. Artists of Florence experimented with foreshortening, with perspective, with the designing of marvelous domes, the making of great bronze doors and singing galleries for their cathedral.

There were wonderful painters, some of them painting formal, majestic pictures, but Fra Filippo was one of those who were content to picture the beauty they saw all around them. They portrayed the Florentine gentlemen and ladies in their proper settings; the pageantry of which the Medici Dukes and the people of Florence were so fond. This fascinating painter-monk, Fra Filippo, was the first to care a great deal about the look of people around him. He painted pictures for the everyday folk to enjoy, believing that their religious message would be conveyed just as clearly, and perhaps even more so. He always painted the Holy Mother like the everyday Florentine mothers he saw in the doorways of their homes, and the Holy Baby like the chubby, dimpled babies the Florentine mothers held in their arms.

Fra Filippo was one of the most human of the early painters, and though his holy pictures were in new, everyday forms, they bore helpful, religious messages just the same.

Filippo Lippi was born in Florence in one of the early years of the fifteenth century, though records do not give us the exact year. While still a child he was placed in the care of the Carmelite Friars, and from them received his education and learned to paint. He joined the Order as a young man but left the convent to follow his career as a painter. He died in 1469 in Spoleto, leaving his son, Filippino Lippi, to inherit his genius and become a great artist like his father.

Some of Filippo Lippi's Pictures:

MADONNA AND CHILD
Uffizi Gallery, Florence
CORONATION OF THE VIRGIN
Uffizi Gallery, Florence
THE ANNUNCIATION
National Gallery of Art, Washington
MADONNA AND CHILD
National Gallery of Art, Washington
MADONNA AND CHILD WITH ANGELS
Metropolitan Museum of Art, New York

FILIPPO, A BOY OF OLD FLORENCE

In a narrow little street in Florence, the City of Flowers, an eight-year-old boy was walking rather slowly and wearily. He had been watching again the tall Bell Tower of Giotto glowing rose and deep gray-green and gold as it soared so lightly up towards the soft blue of the Italian sky, high up above the Cathedral which was waiting to have its marble walls crowned by a great dome.

The boy, Filippo, still saw in his mind the carved pictures on the slender Bell Tower, telling so delicately and beautifully and yet in so real a manner, the story of the labor of men.

"Like a beautiful lily it is," Filippo thought to himself as he walked slowly along. "If only I, too, like the great masters Giotto and Andrea Pisano, could fashion something of beauty for Florence! But I have not the wherewithal for colors or brushes or chisel so that I could show what I can do with my fingers, and perhaps enter the bottega of the great Ghiberti who is planning the bronze pictures for the Baptistery doors. Or if I might enter the workshop of a painter who uses brushes and colors! But Aunt Mona Lapaccia would not understand, and," he nodded his head sagely, "one must have food to make one's fingers make beauty." Ah, food! That was what Filippo wanted most of the time, more than even the fulfillment of the dreams which sometimes came. Oftentimes the hunger which made him faint and dizzy, kept even his eyes from enjoying his beautiful city—all the greater pity, for that pleasure cost not even a soldo! Often when he was not too utterly hungry and lonely, he could forget that hunger and loneliness, as he gazed at the flowers, at the gray and green of the Fiesole hills silvered by the olive trees; or as he listened to a bird's happy song, visited the cathedral where his eyes could feast upon the processions of color and music; or looked long at the delicate Bell Tower and the wonderful carvings which fed his dreams. But when he walked towards his narrow, shabby little street near to the Carmelite convent, past the great houses where he knew that eight-year-old boys had mothers and fathers to care for them, his hunger came rushing back, and sometimes big tears went trickling down from his black eyes, over his thin brown face, making it dirtier than ever. As he wiped them away with a corner of his shabby coat, he would sigh again, and shake his head, more lonely and bewildered the more he tried to reason it out.

There was no use in asking questions of Aunt Mona Lapaccia who had to work so hard to get enough to keep them from starving that she was tired and cross most of the time. Sometimes Filippo could earn a trifle from running an errand for a Florentine master; sometimes a smiling lady threw him a bunch of grapes with which he hurried home as fast as his brown legs would carry him, to share with his aunt. But mostly no one noticed the hungry, dirty, small boy who lingered near the flower stalls, gazed wistfully at the fruit in the open shops, or stole shyly into the cool, dim Cathedral.

"Why have I not a mother and father to love me?" he would often ask himself. "They are dead," Aunt Mona would answer shortly to his timid questions. They had died soon after he was born, and no one had ever told him of them, nor did he have anything which had belonged to them.

When he was not hungry, or cold, or too lonely, there was no boy in Florence who could be more merry. For were there not the sunlight, the green hills and the flowers? To say nothing of music and pictures and the colors he could see all around him. Yes, most days he could find something to bring a twinkle to his dark eyes and a smile to turn up the corners of his mouth. But this day he had not once played a prank to amuse himself; no one had tossed him even a morsel of bread or even a fig or a grape, and he had not earned a penny.

"If only Aunt Mona is not cross and if only she has something to eat," he wished, as he wearily climbed a steep flight of steps which led into a dark, dreary room. But as soon as he entered that room, he knew that his wish was unfulfilled. Aunt Mona sat bent over, her wrinkled, thin, weary face resting in the palms of her hands. She did not look up as Filippo entered. He waited a moment for her to speak and then went slowly to her side, and touched her on the shoulder. "I am hungry," he said plaintively, holding his hands over the place where he felt most faint from the lack of food. "It hurts me here!"

Old Mona Lapaccia raised her head and gazed at him with weary eyes. "Food, always food!" she muttered. "For the sake of my brother Tommaso, have I kept thee, since thou wert a crying and hungry two-year-old. Now thou art owner of eight years, and with each year thou dost grow more hungry, and food more scarce! To the Fathers of the convent of the Carmelites shall I take thee. I can no longer shoulder the burden!"

Filippo longed more than ever for a father and mother to care for him when he found himself in the strange convent with the long stone corridors and the cloisters, all so silent and so different from the noisy and colorful streets of Florence in which he had been accustomed to wander and play and dream, when he wasn't too hungry. True, the convent home was a great improvement in the way of something to eat. Even though his only companions at first were the quiet, solemn monks, and it was all very cold and severe and awesome, even though he still often wished for someone who would care for him as he had seen mothers and fathers care for and love their boys and girls in Florence, yet he was not unhappy, for the Carmelite Fathers were kind to him, his brown robe had no holes, and he was given all the food that he wanted—bread and figs and grapes and olives—everything he had ever wished for! There was the convent garden, too, with its flowers making bright the green just as he had often seen when he peeped through the arched doorways into the gardens of the big, fortresslike houses in the streets of Florence. At first the solemn tones of the convent bell rather frightened him; it was not so mellow and sweet when he heard it from the convent garden, as it had sounded farther off, from his bare little room in the dingy house behind the convent. And although the stone walls of the garden were high, birds could enter and Filippo could still enjoy their songs.

So Filippo was carefree and happy until the Prior determined that he, like the other boys in the convent who were pledged to enter the religious life, must have his lessons in writing, in spelling, in Latin; and he did not like that a bit, although he did like being with other boys.

"Thou art stupid, Filippo," at last cried the friar who had the difficult task of teaching him. "Thou knowest not how to put letters together to form words, and thy Latin! How art thou to become a Carmelite monk if thou canst not read the Latin of our books? Hast thou thought of that?"

Filippo's merry, dark eyes lost their light. "The shapes of the letters I can make with my fingers and I like to make them dance over the page, but to put them together to form a word, spelling, that is more difficult and it interests me not, though I will try, Holy Father, I promise thee!"

Filippo did try, almost bending double over the big books, with a very solemn expression on his small face, which had grown plump and round from good feeding. But give him pencil or pen to copy the exercises the master set him, and behold! The light returned to his eyes until they fairly danced, up turned the corners of his mouth, and so absorbed he became in his work that he had no knowledge of aught that went on around him—not even of the other boys of the convent who crowded around him, fascinated at what he was doing. For Filippo was lost in the joy of drawing odd little figures on the margins of his books; of making funny little images out of the strange letters which formed words—so difficult to put together but so easy to draw with his fingers!

"How is that, Diamante?" he would ask, becoming conscious of his audience as triumphantly he finished a whole big page of quickly drawn little figures, some of them those which had come to his fancy, others caricatures of the boys near whom he sat in class, even sometimes of a monk in his long robe. And they would laugh merrily, until the master himself appeared, all too often before they heard him, and then they would listen to his reproof with lowered heads.

"It is hopeless, Your Reverence," the teacher monk complained to the Prior. "He either will not or cannot apply himself to the learning from books. But give him something to do with his quick-working fingers, then he can see, and understand, and do. Shall I not try him, Reverend Father, in the class of those who copy the beautiful pictures and fine old writing from our holy books?"

The old Friar nodded his head, his hand covering his face for a moment to shut out from the outraged young monk the twinkle which would come to his kindly old eyes, and the smile which threatened to break the composure of his lips.

"Let him have his chance there," he said gently. "Who knows, Fra Albizo, but that thy naughty little friend Filippo will be a credit to thee yet? Who knows but that this Filippo, whose small fingers are so quick in drawing strange little figures in the books where they have no place, may not one day place upon the walls of one of our churches forms of saints and angels which will serve our religion as much as the Latin texts which hold him not? Young Filippo may be to the Carmelite brothers what the gifted Fra Angelico is to the Dominicans. Let him show his skill in copying from our manuscripts, and mayhap watch the miniature artists who follow the cloister-bred Lorenzo Monaco. He leans more towards pattern and rich decoration than our artists of Florence who turn towards Nature for help. Let him study from their work if he shows aptitude, for have we not learned that it is not wrong to paint our Holy Pictures aglow with the beauty of Nature?"

Filippo found a staunch friend in the Prior, who watched his progress with growing interest and amazement. Such delicate lines his small fingers could draw—so that not even the more skeptical Fra Albizo could distinguish any difference between them and the initial letters and border patterns of the manuscript from which he copied. And such beauty of color he could produce—quite as wonderful as the glow of the color in the old books.

"We shall one day have a great painter of our own to decorate our chapel walls," the old Prior would whisper, as he tiptoed away after peeping at Filippo busy at work, and so engrossed in the little picture he was making, that he paid no heed to any who drew near. "It was a good day for us, and we trust for him, when we took him in, a little, half-starved, orphan boy, and gave him a home among us."

The Prior's decree was a very welcome one to Filippo. He was so pleased that he stole out into the convent garden, and as he looked up at the sky flooded with light, he dreamed and planned. He had grown taller during his stay in the convent, and looked well contented with his new home, though sometimes he longed to get out into the big cities.

"I shall become a painter of Holy Pictures," he promised himself and his companion Diamante, and his big brown eyes became as serious as they had sometimes been when he had wandered alone, uncared-for and hungry, through the streets of Florence. Then he had wondered what miracle might happen that he, Filippo, could learn to make the figures of beauty which he felt that his fingers would be able to do. And the miracle had happened!

Then the merry light, which was never banished for long, returned to his eyes, and he smiled broadly, as he chuckled, "But my Holy Pictures shall not be stiff and cold and grand; neither shall they be just beautiful patterns of line and color, full of decoration like some of the beautiful works of Fra Angelico and Lorenzo Monaco, and the early Sienese painters who care not for the study of Nature. Like the carved pictures of Giotto and Andrea Pisano on the fair Bell Tower; like the paintings of Giotto I saw in the dim chapel of a church in Florence; and like the work of the young Masaccio, who, so I have heard the good Prior say, is to paint the pictures on the walls of our Chapel of the Brancacci family, full of beauty of form and warmth and humanness. It is all very well to paint saints and angels and church fathers, but will not all understand the Holy Pictures better, if the figures in them are like those on this earth? If the Holy Mother is like a real mother, caring for her dimpled, plump Bambino?"

Such a splendid opportunity Filippo soon had, the year he was sixteen, of watching the young artist, Masaccio, painting his very real and beautiful pictures on the walls of the convent chapel. Whenever he could be spared, he would steal in to watch the pictures grow, his eager eyes losing not a stroke of the painter's brush, marveling at the glow of color, the beauty of form of the figures, the folds of their drapery, the way the artist grouped his figures in real-looking landscapes which seemed to stretch far away, and the use of light and dark to build up his forms rather than making just patterns of lines.

"So shall my brushes do," murmured Filippo, as day after day he watched, storing away many a rule of painting and the discovery of some new effect of color. "And yet I could never paint pictures so full of dignity, so grand; mine will be for the pleasure and everyday happiness of everyday people."

"*Filippo mio!*" Diamante would cry out in astonishment, "thou canst make figures of an exact likeness to those of the master!"

"It is easy," laughed Filippo, "except for the hands and feet which I never can make behave as they should! But the faces, and the forms, how they flow from the tip of my brush, Diamante. Thou knowest, for thou, too, dost like to draw and paint though thou dost like to make thy figures flat, while I like to make them round with real forms beneath the drapery folds, so that they look to be really there! Come, let us see what we can do in copying this figure of Saint Peter!"

"Did I not tell thee?" the old Prior would triumphantly ask the friars of the Carmelite convent. "The small Filippo was not so impossible as some of you were wont to think," and he wagged a reproachful finger at Fra Albizo. "He has been able to do with his fingers what none of us could do with the help of all the Latin we tried to force him to learn. Now the Carmelites have a painter grown up among them, and when he goes into the world away from the shelter of our chapels and cloisters, away from our teachings which may have reached him through his finger tips rather than through his ears, yet he belongs to us. Listen well to what I now say, my Albizo; even though the expressions on the faces of our Filippo's pictures may be of earth rather than of heaven, yet they will convey their message of religion to the people of Florence, and of whatever cities in which he may work, because of their very humanness. You shall see, Fra Albizo!"

Fra Filippo Lippi did enjoy the world and the everyday people around him, but he painted religious pictures because at the time in which he lived the churches and the convents used Art as their aid in inducing the people to believe their religious teachings; because the rich and important patrons who helped the artists, like the Medici family, added to the beauty of their cities and their own glory by asking artists of the day to decorate the walls of chapels perhaps bearing their names. And of course, Florence wanted to be more beautiful than the other cities around her.

So Fra Filippo painted his love of life as it is with its joys and its sorrows into his religious pictures; beautiful Holy Mothers, no doubt like some gentle, loving mothers he had seen in Florence playing with their chubby babies, in a joyous flower-decorated landscape background. We can almost hear him saying, perhaps to himself,

"I shall paint
God in the midst, Madonna and her Babe,
Ringed by a bowery, flowery angel-brood,
Lilies and vestments and white faces, sweet
As puff on puff of grated orris-root
When ladies crowd to church at Midsummer." *

No doubt news of their gifted pupil, whom they had befriended as a little orphan boy, found its way back to the Fathers of the Carmelite convent. We can almost see one of them, perhaps the kindly, sympathetic old Prior, smiling indulgently as he says:

"Our Filippo has been a match even for the great

* *From Robert Browning's "Men and Women."*

Cosimo de' Medici, I am told. No wonder his paintings have come under the Medici notice, and now our boy is received at his brilliant court. Let us all pray that its splendor and worldliness may not take away the religious teachings we tried to give him here.

"Filippo ever was headstrong and bound to do that which he wished. 'Tis said that our good friend Cosimo did become weary of Filippo's leaving his painting whenever the fancy took him to go out and look upon his fellow beings, so he shut him up in his own palace, telling him he wished him to finish his picture forthwith, and not delay his work by running away at will. One, two, and it may be three days, our headstrong Filippo endured this, and then—I leave thee to tell me what he did!"

"I, too, have heard, Your Worship," smiled one of the friars. "The sheets of his bed he fashioned into a rope by which he escaped from his palace window!"

" 'Twas the Medici who was troubled then," continued the old Prior. "Quickly, he had his painter sought out, promising him freedom to come and go at will, if he would but finish the gracious picture of the Holy Mother and the Angel upon which he had been working. Thou seest, Fra Albizo, what I did tell thee of small Filippo in the old days, holds true now; he, like many others in this world, can be guided by kindness, rather than driven by force. Though Filippo has left us, he will give his message, as he sees it, to the world, and his pictures will become more beautiful and will give happiness not only to the Florence of today but to many who come after his time. Our Filippo who came to us hungry!"

LEONARDO DA VINCI

1452–1519

BEFORE THE STORY

SOMETIMES we become impatient with people who ask a great many questions; but after all, it is a desire to know and understand which prompts these questions. Haven't you ever wanted to find out about a great many things all round you in this great and wonderful world of ours?

Once upon a time there was a boy living in Italy who wanted to know about all things, all the secrets of the earth, the sea, and the sky. He was eager to know all about living things and all about the laws of science which govern the universe. Always he had this inquiring mind, and with it, the eyes to see and the hands to create. He even planned a flying machine two years before Columbus started on his journey across the great waters! So wonderful a man he became that it seems as though there is scarcely a secret he did not solve.

The age he lived in just fitted this great man, Leonardo, for artists at that time were many-sided. Painters were sculptors as well, and often scientists and architects, and sometimes goldsmiths. Leonardo was all these and many more, and he was far in advance of his time in understanding.

He belonged to the Florentine school of artists of which Giotto was the founder, the first of the great Florentine artists to try to make his figures look like real men and women and children and animals, his trees like those he saw around him, his skies blue instead of gold as the earlier artists had pictured them. Leonardo not only knew how to paint and carve and build, but he studied botany, music, poetry, science—almost everything you can think of—and he was filled with enthusiasm for science and for beauty of every kind, a most wonderfully gifted man.

Leonardo da Vinci was born in 1452 in the little Tuscan town of Vinci. As he grew up he was a very clever boy and was given an excellent education and apprenticed to the master artist, Verrocchio. Much of his most important work was done in Milan, where he lived for many years, but his famous "Mona Lisa" was painted during a four years' stay in Florence. He became court painter to King Louis XII of France and later to Francis I. He died in 1519 in France, after a long, brilliant and happy career, an unusual genius in an age of geniuses.

Some of Leonardo's Paintings and Drawings:

DRAWINGS, PORTRAIT STUDIES, CARICATURES
  Accademia di Belle Arte, Venice
LAST SUPPER
  Refectory of Santa Maria delle Grazie, Milan
MADONNA, CHILD, AND SAINT ANNE
  Louvre, Paris
MONA LISA OR LA GIACONDA
  Louvre, Paris

THE MAGICIAN PAINTER: LEONARDO

An Artist Who Tried to Invent a Flying Machine

In the little town of Vinci, high up among great rocks crowning a steep hillside, about twenty miles from Florence, was born over four hundred years ago, Leonardo, son of Ser Piero d'Antonio of Vinci, a lawyer. He was a strange boy, more beautiful than most children, with hair the color of gold and soft as spun silk. His eyes were of a deep clear blue, with a strange light in them. No one in the little village could withstand his smile, and he was a great favorite with all, especially with the boys and the girls, for he could invent such wonderful games!

As Leonardo grew older, he was sent to school, but he did not like that a bit, not he! "Oh, Mother Catarina," he would complain, "I care not about the Latin Grammar I am taught by the master. Arithmetic is well enough, though I would ask many more questions than pleases our teacher. I want to find out all about living things, the spiders, the butterflies, and the birds!"

But when one day he saw some rough boys tearing off butterfly wings, he turned very white and ran away from them as swiftly as possible. Away up into the hills he liked to go, where he could breathe the sweet, fresh air, and find out about the things he wished to know, and he wanted to find out the hidden reason of all things. He loved to watch a spider weaving its web of delicate threads, the beautifully colored butterflies, the funny sounding bees, but more than all he loved to watch the birds.

"If only I had wings and could fly like the swallows, Mother Catarina," the little Leonardo used to say; "just to think of being able to sail through the clear air, with that lovely dipping motion! Way up into the clouds I would go, high above the tallest cypress tree on the highest mountain!"

"Perhaps if I watch them long enough, I, too, will learn how to fly," he often thought, standing on a hilltop and trying to make motions of flying like the birds he saw. "Ah, I almost have it! My arms must stretch out at the sides like wings to press back the air! All ready, here I go!" he would cry joyfully, only to roll down the hillside till he stopped himself by clutching at the roots of a good strong shrub!

It was far easier to imitate the songs of the birds than their flying and he would listen long to their sweet music, to the murmuring of the brooks and the soft sighing of the wind in the treetops, until the love of music began to take possession of him. Often he would stand for a very long time, watching the dark green foliage of the olive trees turn to a silvery gray as the breeze swayed the delicate leaves, and then he would play and through the music, he would dream of the great things he was going to do. When, to his joy, a lute was given him, he played upon it the music which came to his mind and his heart, wild, strangely sweet songs, with rich, mellow tones of a marvelous clearness. Everyone in the little town of Vinci would stop to listen when they heard his songs and the children would gather around him and follow him wherever he went, for there was a magic in his music which they could not resist. He was the Pied Piper of Vinci.

When the boy was thirteen years of age, his father decided he must learn some definite work. "Our son must study some trade, Catarina," he said. But he could do so many things well that it was hard to decide which one he should choose, though his love for drawing was perhaps the most keen. At that time there was in Florence, to which city they had moved and where Ser Piero practiced law, a painter and sculptor and a very good teacher of painting and carving and drawing, by the name of Verrocchio. He lived near to the bridge across the Arno river, called the Ponte Vecchio. So Ser Piero, Leonardo's father, went to Florence and showed Verrocchio some of his son's drawings.

A fine workshop had Verrocchio. There was the outer room, where the marble was chipped into statues, the room where fine carvings were done, and panels of wood were made ready for painting; and the inner workshop where the statues made from beautiful marble and the paintings were kept free from dust. There, the modeling in wax of little statues could be kept from dirt, and the gold and silver work treasured. For Andrea Verrocchio was a goldsmith, as well as a sculptor, an architect, a painter. He was even a designer of banners when they were needed for the celebration of some famous dignitary in the city of Florence.

"Dost think thou canst make aught of the boy?" Ser-Piero asked anxiously as they looked at the sketches he had brought.

At first, Andrea Verrocchio scarcely looked at the drawings, as he held them carelessly in his hand.

"Alas!" he sighed, shaking his head. "Our city of Florence is filled with fathers who think their boys can draw, and of boys who think themselves artists!" Then he looked more closely at his handful of drawings. There were butterflies flying, strange kinds of birds and birdlike machines with great wings stretching out, studies of flowers and animals, plans of churches and lighthouses, engines of war.

"Oh-ho!" he cried in surprise. "Send the boy to me at once! He has real talent! How firm that line, and what beauty in the curve of this one! Your son knows how to use his pencil and will soon know how to use his brush. What an eye he has for observing! Send the boy to me at once. One day the Medici will be asking work from him."

So Leonardo entered Verrocchio's workshop as a pupil, and all who saw his work exclaimed over it in wonder and delight.

At first Leonardo found plenty to do in just watching Verrocchio and his well-trained assistants in their busy workshop. How it hummed and buzzed with work all the busy day! Some were busy casting a great bell for the cathedral; others were finishing a silver candlestick for a nearby church; while the master himself was working on the figure of an angel in a painting. Then Leonardo, too, began to work, copying from his master's works, and helping him in some of the details of his pictures.

One day the bottega door opened and three tall young men stood on the threshold. Leonardo knew that they must be some very grand gentlemen, for Verrocchio, his master, bowed before them. Many a time had he been commissioned to paint tournament banners, plan decorations for their festivities, as well as fulfil commissions for beautiful paintings and statues. For the Medici Dukes loved beautiful things, and helped the artists of Florence in making their city beautiful.

"Welcome, your Excellencies!" he cried. "Come, let your Worships tell me what you think of my Holy Picture. Behold, my brush has just sent the soft evening light into the sky against which the cypresses stand, and turned the distant mountain tops into silver!"

After the Medici Dukes had admired and criticized Verrocchio's work, the master sent Leonardo, who had been standing quietly in a corner of the inner workshop, on an errand.

"Look, your Excellencies!" he urged, "at the drawings my new pupil has made. Are they not full of promise?"

"Even so, Andrea," answered Lorenzo. "Keep an eye on that boy, for Florence has need of more artists!"

"Never fear, your Magnificence," promised Verrocchio. "Even now I have given him the figure of the kneeling angel in my new picture to draw; if he does well, then shall he paint it upon the canvas. But, your Excellencies, the boy is too wonderful; he aims at too great perfection, and wants to know too many things. He wants to know everything and to do everything, and life is not long enough for that! Never will he work long at one thing, though he is never idle. Sometimes, instead of painting, he will carve little toys of people which can move their arms and legs, to amuse the other lads in my workshop. Sometimes he takes caged birds to the market place, and sets them free to watch them fly, for he says that one day he will make a machine which shall fly through the air like a bird! He is a very strange boy."

"Who knows?" murmured Lorenzo the Magnificent, with a faraway look. "Who knows but that one day we shall fly through the air like a bird? But tell the lad from me not to waste his precious time on these toys and neglect his painting. Tell him we shall visit this workshop soon again."

When Verrocchio told Leonardo what the Medici Duke had said, he set him straightway to work on the figure of the kneeling angel. For just a moment Leonardo hesitated, with a thoughtful look in his eyes. Then he took his brushes and colors, and with quick, sure strokes began to paint. Not once did he stop until the kneeling angel was finished. When Verrocchio looked at the work which his pupil had done, he knew that the boy was one day bound to rise far above him.

"I have found my master," murmured he to himself, laying his hand gently on the lad's shoulder.

But Leonardo hardly seemed to hear. Seldom did he notice when people praised or blamed him, so eager was he to solve all sorts of new problems.

Ser Piero, his father, was very proud of his son's success in Verrocchio's studio, so, when one morning a peasant who worked on his estate, asked him to have a design painted on a wooden shield which he had, Ser Piero granted his request, thinking to himself, "My Leonardo shall try his hand at it! Thus shall I save money and find out what he can do." Accordingly he took the shield to his son in Verrocchio's workshop.

Leonardo was delighted with the request. It was just the sort of thing he liked to do. First, he held it to the fire to straighten it, for it was badly shaped. Then he sent it to a turner to be smoothed. When it was all carefully shaped and smoothed, he sat down to plan what he should paint upon it. "Shall I paint the dainty violets I saw only yesterday? Or a white-winged bird, or mayhap a figure of victory!" Leonardo loved to draw strange monsters, so he said to himself gleefully, "Nay, I have it! something which will give surprise to the owner of this shield, and to my father, too."

He went hastily out, alone, and collected all the strangest creatures he could find: lizards, snakes, and bats, and took them secretly to his own workroom. Then, allowing no one to enter, he began to paint from them a most curious and terrible monster, half dragon and half bat! When it was finished he hung the shield against a heavy dark curtain, with the light falling full upon it, so that it stood out in very strong relief, and looked as if it were really alive, and just about to twist and writhe and spread its hideous wings!

There came a knock at the door, and Ser Piero stood outside. "Is my shield ready?" he asked, anxious to see what his son had made. "I will take it with me to my workman."

"Come in, Father," cried Leonardo, his eyes twinkling as he wondered what his father would say to this strange creature he had made.

Ser Piero glanced at the strange monster he saw seeming to be just ready to spring at him, with fire darting from its eyes and smoke from its nostrils. Then, uttering a cry of alarm, he started to run out of the room!

"Come back!" Leonardo laughed, catching hold of his cloak. "Look closer and you will see that my dragon will not hurt you! But if I have frightened you, I have made a convincing dragon. Take this to your workman. It will frighten off his foes, even as the Gorgon's head aided the Greek hero, Perseus!"

His father could scarcely believe that it was only a painting and still approached it rather cautiously. So proud was he of his son's work, that he kept that shield and gave the peasant another!

Finally Leonardo grew restless in Verrocchio's studio. He had studied under him, he had learned from Botticelli, from the works of Ghirlandajo and from the Pollaiuolo brothers, who had dipped deep into the secrets of anatomy—how the human body is put together—and of perspective—the art of giving the feeling of distance in a picture. Now he wanted to go out into the world and create something of his own. Sometimes he would stand gazing at the graceful bell tower designed by Giotto, and as he looked at its delicate beauty against the soft evening sky, he would plan to make something as beautiful. Sometimes, among the trees and flowers of the courtyard of San Marco, he dreamed of wonderful things he himself would one day accomplish.

The master, Verrocchio, was modeling a statue of the brave Venetian general, Bartolomeo Colleoni, who had left his fortune to Venice, with the request that they erect a statue in his honor. Leonardo watched him at his work. He, too, studied the drawings of the great equestrian statue of the Roman Emperor, Marcus Aurelius, which Donatello had made for Rome. He, too, made many sketches of horses at rest and horses in action. So, when he learned that Duke Lodovico Sforza of Milan was searching for a sculptor who would commemorate his father, by an equestrian statue, he determined to compete for the honor of making the statue.

"Get for me the commission to make this great statue, O master," begged Leonardo. "I promise you that my master shall not feel ashamed of me."

"Show His Magnificence, Duke Lorenzo, the new silver lute your fingers have fashioned, the next time he visits our bottega," Verrocchio suggested. "That will create in him an interest in you, for its form is well made and its tone deep and sweet. He is a friend of the Duke of Milan."

Lorenzo de' Medici drew his long, scarlet cloak closely around his shoulders, and leaned back to listen amazedly to the young Leonardo, who was playing upon his silver lute.

"Bravissimo!" he cried; "I will send young Leonardo to Milan, as my messenger to the Duke Lodovico. He shall play upon his lute for him, for I doubt whether any other can play upon it as well as he. I would, however, that he send to him a letter, telling him of the many kinds of work that he can do."

So Leonardo gladly set out for Milan, breathing more

freely as he went out into the world. Before starting, however, he wrote to the Duke of Milan telling him just what he could do, and there was hardly anything that Leonardo could not do! He told him how useful he could be to him in war and in peace; he could write both prose and poetry, make bridges, dig canals, invent a new kind of cannon, build warships, design houses, make statues, paint pictures, and produce sweet music! This letter was a very curious one, for it was written from right to left, and with his left hand as Leonardo always wrote, so that the only way it could be read was by holding the writing up before a mirror.

"What manner of man is this Leonardo?" the amazed Lodovico asked. "Such a strange letter! How could any man do what he claims he can? Listen, while I read to you what he says. I will read or tell you portions from it.

" 'If by reason of the elevation or the strength of its position a place cannot be bombarded, I can demolish every fortress if its foundations have not been set on stone.' He says that he can construct my public buildings, invent engines of war, make beautiful sculpture, cast works in bronze, paint to my satisfaction. Moreover, he claims to have designed and executed—and our ears tell us that he can play—the beautiful lute of silver my good friend Lorenzo of Florence sent to me. Its richness of tone is unsurpassed. Truly, he is a strange man, and the letter a strange one, written from right to left and with his left hand. Either he is a man of genius or a fool! But he shall have the commission for the statue of my honored father on his horse's back. *Bene!* He can do no more than fail, as other artists have done before him."

Everyone in Milan liked Leonardo: princes, noblemen, ladies, artists, writers, philosophers. A black velvet cap upon his golden hair, a cloak of dark red cloth thrown across his shoulders, his clear eyes sparkling and his friendly smile ready, he could often be seen talking in the public squares with the learned men of his day. Often he was a guest at the great banquets. Wherever he might be, he would frequently stop to put down a note or make a sketch in his notebook which he always had with him. And many and varied were the works which Leonardo began to carry out. Always he was working on his model for the bronze statue of the Duke's father upon his horse's back. For years he worked on his painting of the Last Supper for the dining room of Santa Maria delle Grazie in Milan.

Year after year he worked at the great painting. Sometimes, unable to get the result he wished, he would leave it for weeks or months and then return to it and try again. Sometimes he would paint from the time the sun first warmed the eastern sky, to the time when it sank in all its radiance at the end of its journey in the west. Those were the days when Leonardo did not lay down his brushes for food or drink, and his very heart sang because of the inspiration which came. Though never could he make it as he wished it to be. He would stand long gazing at what he had done, and then, dissatisfied, go to try his skill on another great work, thinking to return with renewed vigor to the one he had left.

Always, he remembered his desire to learn the secret art of flying, and every once in a while he would try a new scheme. "In my own mind I can see it clearly," he would tell to his wondering friends. "Like a great bird with outstretched wings sailing and dipping through the clear air; now low, now high and higher towards the deep blue. One day there will surely be a birdlike ship which shall fly through the air. Thus it is bound to be. It is only a question of knowing how to make the form of the ship and the wings, and most important of all, the spark that shall make them go. All my life I seem to be talking and planning about wings!"

The great painting of the Last Supper grew and grew until it was almost finished. But unfortunately the Duke was obliged to flee before the French soldiers who invaded Milan; some careless monks, later, cut a door through the center of the picture, and the dampness in the wall dimmed the colors. But still there is enough of it to make us stand in awe and wonder before the genius of the great Leonardo.

It was back again in Florence that he painted the world-famed portrait of Mona Lisa, the wife of a Florentine gentleman, Francesco del Giocondo.

"Behold, Madonna! Thy portrait shall one day please all the world!" Leonardo would prophesy. "Four years have I worked, and at last I have caught thy spirit, the soul which looks out through thine eyes. Smile once again, as the music pleases thee, that I may imprison it for the many years to come, for the enjoyment of numberless people.

" 'My Lady looks, and from her shining eyes
Gleams forth her soul, . . .
My Lady speaks, and on her lips the while, . . .
There lies the image of her soul—a smile.' " *

Leonardo became the court painter of King Francis the First of France. Often he would sit before a glowing fire, on a winter evening, in the splendid castle which the King had given him, and think of his unfulfilled dreams, his unfinished works. He would look over his sketchbook filled with the many drawings he had made of men and

* *From A. J. Anderson's "The Admirable Painter." A Study of Leonardo da Vinci.*

women, young and old; beautiful ones and homely ones, those sad and those merry, for all faces interested him. It was not many years, however, before his hand was unable to hold a pencil or brush, and in 1519, one day in the spring-time, when the trees were showing forth their delicate green and gray, when the soft white clouds were floating across the blue of the sky, Leonardo died. He was a genius not only as a painter and sculptor, but in his inventions as well. As an architect, poet, musician, philosopher, scientist, Leonardo was the most wonderful man and capable of accomplishing more great things than any other of his time, a universal genius. Leonardo, himself, said, "As a well-spent day brings happy sleep, so life, well used, brings happy death."

ALBRECHT DÜRER

1471–1528

BEFORE THE STORY

THE FOLK of the quaint little town of Nuremberg, the first famous art center of Germany, are prouder of Albrecht Dürer than of any other of their artists. There, as a boy in his father's goldsmith shop, he fashioned out of clay little figures which were afterwards cast in metal, an excellent training for one who later carved in wood.

What a fascinating place for Albrecht to live in as a boy! The old city of Nuremberg had round towers and turrets in the protecting wall, three hundred and sixty-five of them! There were, and still are, gabled houses almost like toy houses, a moat, or broad, deep ditch filled with water, to keep the enemy away, plenty of brown houses with red-tiled roofs, and flowering plants in the windows. The houses in the old part of the city almost meet across the narrow and often winding streets, and quaint, old, lofty-spired churches, with their pointed doors and windows, give added charm to Nuremberg.

In the busy shops carvers of Nuremberg created gay little figures out of wood, toys to please the boys and girls, spears for the Crusaders, or Soldiers of the Cross, watches, altars and Holy Images for those altars. It was a prosperous town in the Middle Ages, an art center. From the clay banks fine pottery was modeled, sculptors designed splendid fountains for the public squares, and musicians, painters, cobblers, master workmen all, contributed to the many arts which flourished. There were wealthy merchants who were patrons of the arts, eager to gratify their love of beauty and importance.

Although Albrecht Dürer lived in this town, which still seems to belong to the Middle Ages, as long ago as the days of Christopher Columbus, we can still find his gabled house on a very narrow street close beneath the high, towered castle, all looking very much like a picture from a very old book.

No doubt the young Albrecht used to listen to the Mastersingers of Nuremberg, groups of wonderful singers from everyday working people—tailors, shoemakers, bakers, armorers, potters, woodcarvers—all very devoted to music. No doubt he grew as excited as the rest of the folk when the contests took place to see whether the singers might win the title of Mastersinger, which was a very great honor indeed. One Mastersinger was more famous and better loved than any other—Hans Sachs the cobbler-poet, who wrote so many songs and who was a Mastersinger for nearly sixty years. In the famous opera by Richard Wagner, "The Mastersingers of Nuremberg," Hans Sachs is the leading character.

Our poet, Mr. Longfellow, wrote about this interesting old town:

> "Quaint old town of toil and traffic,
> Quaint old town of art and song,
> Memories haunt thy pointed gables,
> Like the rooks that round them throng.
>
> Through these streets so broad and stately,
> These obscure and dismal lanes,
> Walked of yore the Mastersingers,
> Chanting rude poetic strains."

No town in Germany or Italy is more unchanged than is Nuremberg, so we can all the more vividly picture the home and surroundings of its greatest artist, this Albrecht Dürer, who grew in importance until he became favorite of an Emperor, the mighty Maximilian.

How Albrecht loved to draw! Soon he made up his mind that he wanted to become a painter rather than a goldsmith. So, when he was fifteen years old, he was apprenticed to Master Wohlgemuth, the best painter and sculptor to be found in Nuremberg at that time. From him Albrecht learned a great deal about color and wood engraving.

How real are Albrecht Dürer's Holy Pictures! His Holy Mothers and Babies are like everyday German mothers and plump, happy babies. How exquisitely all the tiniest details are finished, every bit of them, hands, hair, expression, and all quite true to Nature. Not only did he paint pictures but he engraved them, and did a great deal to further book pictures. The many fine, realistic woodcuts he designed made it possible to illustrate books for the very first time.

The Emperor Maximilian visited Nuremberg, and was so pleased with this artist that he wanted him to make pictures in his honor. Think of it! Dürer made ninety-two separate blocks of woodcuts for the engraved pictures honoring the Emperor, and arranged them in the form of a great arch. In that same poem on Nuremberg by Longfellow, are these words about this artist:

"Here, where Art was still religion, with a simple, reverent heart,
Lived and labored Albrecht Dürer, the Evangelist of Art; . . .

Dead he is not, but departed,—for the artist never dies,
Fairer seems the ancient city, and the sunshine seems more fair,
That he once has trod its pavement, that he once has breathed its air!"

Dürer's great friend in Nuremberg, Wilebald Pirkheimer, said of him, "He united every virtue in his soul —genius, uprighteousness, purity, energy and prudence, gentleness and piety."

Some of Dürer's Paintings and Drawings:

ADORATION OF THE MAGI
Uffizi Gallery, Florence
SELF PORTRAIT
Prado Museum, Madrid
THE EMPEROR MAXIMILIAN (*charcoal drawing*)
Albertina Museum, Vienna
A HARE (*water-color drawing*)
Albertina Museum, Vienna
MADONNA AND CHILD WITH SAINT ANNE
Metropolitan Museum of Art, New York
VIRGIN AND CHILD
Metropolitan Museum of Art, New York
MADONNA WITH A PEAR (*engraving*)
Vassar College Art Gallery, Poughkeepsie
THE WIFE OF JOBST PLANCKFELT
Museum of Art, Toledo, Ohio

MAXIMILIAN'S FAVORITE PAINTER: ALBRECHT DÜRER OF NUREMBERG

"Isn't it strange, Andrew, that only three of us eighteen children lived to grow up?" Young Albrecht stood in his father's goldsmith shop in Nuremberg, the sunlight shining upon his fair hair as he craned his neck and stood on his toes that he might the better see himself in the rather small and unsatisfactory mirror upon the wall. "You, Hans and I are left and all the rest are gone!"

"Whatever set you to thinking about that, Albrecht?" questioned his older brother, Andrew, who had just finished lowering the shutters at the windows and getting things in order for the day. "You would better be helping me with the making of this gold cup as our father showed us, than looking at yourself in the mirror! Come, Albrecht, the metal is ready to be heated."

"In a moment's time, Andrew," murmured Albrecht dreamily, standing still finally and peering at himself very intently through the mirror. "Now I am ready."

"Ready for what, Albrecht?" asked Hans, the oldest of the three Dürer boys, running down the narrow stairs leading from the room above. "Are you getting yourself ready for festivities at the castle that you are admiring yourself so intently?"

"Fortunate it is, indeed," sighed thirteen-year-old Albrecht, the youngest of the three boys, "that our fifteen brothers and sisters did not live! Then my life would have been miserable indeed! If you must know, my two curious brothers, I am making a likeness of myself as I see my reflection through the mirror."

"Of all things, Albrecht!" cried the amazed and almost

horrified Hans. "Whatever would our father say?"

"Better finish your task of melting the gold, Albrecht," advised Andrew, beginning to polish the gold and silver dishes which were finished, and then to cover them so that not a speck of dust could reach them. "Your reflection in the mirror will come any time you call it forth."

"But look, Andrew! Hans, do come here! I worked on this last night after you two and Father thought I was in bed. I need daylight to finish it. See, here on this paper. 'I have portrayed this after my own image' in my thirteenth year."

"Albrecht!" cried the amazed Andrew, letting fall one of his tools with a clatter to the floor, as he and Hans went close to look. "It is a splendid likeness, the real you! Whatever will our father say?"

"And what will our mother say?" laughed Barbara Dürer, their mother, briskly entering the goldsmith's shop. "Thou hast made thy very image! Though I know not what thy father will think."

"That I should pay greater heed to the art of the goldsmith, no doubt," sighed Albrecht as he put away his pencils. "But I'll never be as good a goldsmith as I will be a painter or a draughtsman. Now, you have my ambition!"

"The goldsmith's art is good enough for me," declared Andrew rather sternly. "What about you, Hans?"

Hans looked rather guilty. "I am with Albrecht in this. I, too, want to become a painter."

"I know not what your father will say, for he has labored to teach you his art. Andrew, I am glad you have the desire to become a goldsmith like your father. As for Hans and Albrecht, I would that you do that which is in your hearts. All I ask is that in whatever you do you love God and be kind to those with whom you have to deal. But it is my advice that you will tell your father at once and humbly ask him to help you in apprenticing you to painters who will help you in your chosen craft. Who knows but that one of you will bring honor to him and to Nuremberg?"

In Nuremberg there were many master craftsmen—Adam Kraft, the sculptor, who carved a shrine for the Church of Saint Sebald; Veit Stoss, the well-known carver in wood; Michael Wohlgemuth, a painter and sculptor. To the latter Albrecht was sent when he was fifteen years old, apprenticed to him for three years, learning much about color and also about wood engraving, but he was not so very happy. "How can I be, my father? The Master's men, who are much older than I, do not like to have me here, and are most unkind. When my term of service is over, I'd like to go to Colmar and enter the Schongauer workshop."

"First, my son," his father admonished him, "I would have you go out into the world studying and working as you go. One day you must go to the land of great painters in line and in color, to beautiful Italy, where you will see the work of such Masters as you have never dreamed were in the world. It will do more than anything else to help you in your chosen work."

A carver in wood and in ivory, a sculptor, a painter, engraver, and a writer and poet, too! Like the great Leonardo of Italy, there was scarcely anything he could not do! And like Leonardo, he was a great thinker. Everything he undertook seemed, through his understanding, to turn into a beautiful work of art.

He wrote to his brothers while upon a later visit to Venice, "How I love this beautiful, sunny land! Old Giovanni Bellini has praised my work in the presence of many noblemen. That is a great deal coming from him who is still one of the best of the painters of Italy. His pupils, the young Giorgione and Titian, young though they be, are Masters in light and shadow and color. I see them at their work decorating the outer walls of our new Exchange of German Merchants as I go inside to work on the altarpiece for the new chapel. How I wish you were all here in this sunny land to see the pictures by these Italian artists, and to meet my many good friends who warn me against those who copy my work and then go about saying that the style is not good! Hans, I wish you were here with me in Venice where you could learn the language, study the masterpieces, and be helpful to me. So you would be, had not our dear mother been loth to let you go, fearing that the sky would fall down upon you! How you would love this land! When I leave I shall 'freeze after this sun,' and how I shall miss the color in the sea, the sunsets, the people—especially the jolly pipers and dancers and lute players. And here I have more orders for pictures than I can carry out. Yet I long for my beloved Nuremberg which I shall never forget."

So carefully did Albrecht Dürer hold the brush and so accurately did he use it that he could paint upon his canvas or panel of wood even the most detailed subject, without sketching it beforehand. "It is wonderful!" declared the most distinguished of painters. "That is a very difficult thing to do."

"My good friend Albrecht," one day said the old Master, Giovanni Bellini, of Venice, "I marvel at the fineness and delicacy of your admirable drawings of hair. That reminds me, Albrecht, will you gratify a whim of mine?"

"You have only to ask me, good Messere Bellini, and it shall be granted, anything that I can do for you."

"Then make me a present of one of the brushes with which you picture hairs."

"Here is one, Master, and here are others, just like all the other brushes as you will see. In fact, if I mistake not, they are like the brushes you use in painting your unrivaled portraits. Take whichever one you wish, or take them all, if you would like them."

"Nay, friend Albrecht, you must have misunderstood. I meant the brushes with which you 'draw several hairs with one stroke; they must be rather spread out and more divided, otherwise in a long sweep such regularity of curvature and distance would not be preserved.' "

"I have made no mistake, good Master Giovanni; I use no other brushes than these. See, I will prove it to you!"

Thereupon, Dürer took up one of the brushes and with it quickly drew upon his canvas a woman's long, wavy hair.

"I never would have believed it," declared the old Venetian Master, "had I not seen it with my own eyes!"

Back in Nuremberg Dürer found plenty of orders awaiting him, and busied himself with his painted and engraved pictures all the day long. So many pictures he was asked to make that he needed apprentices to help him, just as he had once served as an apprentice boy in other workshops. And you may be sure he kept them all busy, sweeping the workshop, cleaning his brushes, grinding his colors, making ready wood blocks, for his woodcut pictures. Then a very exciting event took place. The Emperor Maximilian visited Nuremberg!

"The Emperor, Kaiser Max, has come to live in our castle!" cried the excited folk of Nuremberg. "We must do our best to please him, and since he is so fond of the fine arts, we are fortunate indeed in having Albrecht Dürer. Who knows but what the Emperor will ask him to paint his portrait? Then our Albrecht's fortune would be made! But he will have to work hard to please, for has not Kaiser Max been known to say, 'I am a king of kings'?"

"You indeed please me, Albrecht Dürer," declared the Emperor, often visiting the painter's studio. "And if you keep on pleasing me you shall be made court painter. Straightway I commission you to make a triumphal arch in my honor; not one which must remain in one city or town like those which glorified the Emperors of Rome, but one which will travel with me. You shall make woodcut pictures telling the story of my life. Then, my Albrecht, when they are arranged in the form of a gigantic arch, will it not surpass the triumphal arch of any other ruler?"

So Dürer set to work upon the Emperor's monument, a triumphal arch which could be folded up, and taken wherever he might go, to please his vanity. Ninety-two woodcuts he made, which, when joined together, formed an arch of pictures nine feet wide and a little over ten feet high. He painted his portrait, too, and decorated a Book of Hours, a religious book, with ever so many quaint little drawings of delightful little animals, and decorative ornaments.

One day, when Dürer was working for his Emperor, no doubt one of the days when he was painting his portrait, Maximilian, or "Prince Max" as the painter called him, took up a piece of charcoal and tried to draw with it as the painter did. With a vigorous grasp, he tried to make a stroke—but the charcoal broke in his hand! Again he tried, each time with the same result. "Most gracious Emperor," said Albrecht Dürer, "I would not that your Majesty should draw so well as I do! . . . I am practiced in this, and it is my province; thou, Emperor, hast harder tasks and another calling." About his charcoal drawing of the Emperor, now in the Albertina, Vienna, he wrote, "This is the Emperor Maximilian, whose likeness I, Albrecht Dürer, have taken at Augsburg, high up in the palace in his little chamber, in the year of Grace 1518, on Monday after St. John the Baptist's Day."

Hans Sachs, the cobbler-poet told about so vividly in the famous opera about the Mastersingers of Nuremberg by Richard Wagner, lived there during a part of Dürer's lifetime, and so the cobbler-poet, when he was getting together his group of Mastersingers, must have known the artist who had won fame in other cities, but returned to his home city of Nuremberg, to honor it with his painter's gift. No doubt the cobbler-poet had rejoiced with the other townsfolk when the Emperor honored Albrecht with his favor. No doubt he said with the others, "Think of it! One of our Nuremberg folk, Albrecht Dürer, our great artist, has been asked to paint the portrait of Kaiser Max, and 'tis rumored that he will be made court painter!"

Likewise, the busy painter must have been present at some midsummer festival when the Mastersingers contended. Having been an apprentice in his father's goldsmith shop, he would have been interested in the goldsmiths' guild, as well as the painters' and engravers' guilds, the members of which must all have rejoiced over such a famous son of Nuremberg. Hans Sachs may have sat to him for his portrait, as did many of the burghers.

So, on one of the music festival days, we can easily picture the painter marching with the other members of his guild, joining in their songs, as they entered the Nuremberg meadows. Shoemakers, tailors, bakers, sculptors, goldsmiths, painters, mastersingers, all appeared in holiday attire with the regalia of their guilds, banners waving, all joining in the song.

"Hans Sachs, Hans Sachs!" cried the boys and girls with whom the cobbler was a great favorite. And they danced about him.

"Albrecht Dürer, Albrecht Dürer!" cried the people.

Many of them had had their portraits painted or engraved by him, and marveled at the wonderful likenesses which came from his pencil and brush.

Eagerly the cobbler-poet and the artist watched and listened. They watched when the singers who had been admitted to the Mastersingers contended for the honor of receiving the silver chain with its three silver medals, one of them having carved on it the head of King David of Judea, who was said to be the first Mastersinger. One after another, the contestants mounted the green mound which had been erected for a platform, and sang their songs to the applause or the laughter of the people. Albrecht Dürer cheered with the rest when the best singer received the silver chain.

Fond of travel and adventure, always, he was glad of the need of going to the Netherlands to find the new Emperor, Charles the Fifth, Maximilian's successor, that he might discover whether he would confirm the grant of a pension for his services as court painter. This amusing story has come down to us of an adventure on that journey. He had heard of a tremendous whale which had been washed up on one of the Dutch shores and straightway hurried to see it. On the way, he passed flooded lands where only the roofs of the houses appeared above the waters. A large ship ran against his smaller boat just as he was about to go on shore. The ropes broke, and before they could land or the sailors return to the boat, they were cast adrift. Only Dürer himself, a friend of his from Nuremberg, two women, a boy and the boatman, were left on board. A hurricane overtook them and sent them seaward. The wind was so severe and the sea so rough that none of the sailors on shore dared go to their aid. Dürer calmed his frightened companions and with the boatman's help managed to raise a small sail, so that they might get ashore again. But by the time they reached the shore where the whale was said to be, it had been washed away!

In a famous age lived the artist, Albrecht Dürer, an age of inventions and discoveries, of Caxton and the printing press, of Columbus and the new lands westward; of great masters of Italy whose pictures have been studied by artists of all lands. Dürer, like one of these artists, the many-sided Leonardo, had the inquiring mind which belonged to that time, and combined with it a strong feeling of reality and understanding of beauty.

MICHELANGELO

1475–1564

BEFORE THE STORY

THERE are many kinds of picture books besides those we commonly think of when we say those words. There are the great cathedrals built in the Middle Ages, with their builders, sculptors, painters, makers of the windows of colored glass, giving to them their very best, and really creating great picture books for the everyday folk who could afford no books written by hand and decorated by glowing little pictures. However, they could go day after day to enjoy the carved and painted holy pictures in these beautiful churches.

The great Michelangelo was a sculptor first of all but he was also an architect and a painter, so much interested in the human form that he gave his painted figures the appearance of having been modeled. On the ceiling of the Sistine Chapel belonging to the Church of St. Peter in Rome, he painted many, many Bible stories—a Gigantic Picture Book—and the mighty Michelangelo was surely a giant among artists.

Let us get acquainted with the boy, Michelangelo, and the man, so that we will better understand Michelangelo the wonderful artist whose works, painted and carved, will always live.

Michelangelo Buonarroti was born in 1475 at Caprese near Florence and at an early age, while apprenticed to the great artist Ghirlandajo, won the attention and praise of the Medici dukes, the great Florentine patrons of art.

He loved Florence and lived most of his life there, though he was forced to spend several years in Rome at work on his gigantic paintings in the Sistine Chapel, in carving a tomb for Pope Julius II and in designing the great Church of St. Peter with its wonderful gilded dome.

Michelangelo was a rather lonely man, living by himself. He often said that his art took the place of a wife and children, but we wonder if he was not sometimes very lonesome. One friend made his days happier, a very wonderful woman, Vittoria Colonna, to whom he has written sonnets.

Some of Michelangelo's Works:

Holy Family
  Uffizi Gallery, Florence
Bible Pictures on the Ceiling of the Sistine Chapel
  Rome
Statue of Moses (*for tomb of Pope Julius*)
  Church of S. Pietro in Vincoli, Rome
Statue of David
  Academy, Florence
Study for Delphic Sibyl (*drawing*)
  Metropolitan Museum of Art, New York

THE GIGANTIC PICTURE BOOK OF MICHELANGELO

Lodovico di Lionardo Buonarroti Simoni ("My, what a mouthful of names!" I can hear you saying) was a very proud man on the morning of March the sixth, over four hundred years ago, for a new boy baby had just been born to him, whom he decided to name Michelangelo. "Who knows but what this tiny boy will make himself famous in our beautiful city of Florence? May he grow into a learned man, a scholar, whose writings will be so full of wise sayings that even the Medici dukes will learn from them!"

It would be the height of good fortune to win the interest and help of the Medici duke, Lorenzo, who was such a great and important man that he was called "The Magnificent." He wanted his city of Florence to be more beautiful and more wonderful than any other city of Italy, and so was glad to encourage all the young men who had something to offer which would add to its fame and the beauty of his City of Flowers.

When Michelangelo was about six months old, he was given into the care of a nurse in a little village not far from Florence where his father owned a farm. More people in that little village and those nearby earned their living in the stone quarries than by tilling the soil. The baby boy with the long name, Michelangelo, had for his nurse, or foster mother, the daughter of a stonecutter. So he was brought up with the gigantic stones greeting his eyes every day, and the sound of the chisels and the hammers ringing in his ears.

"I am spending my time studying the Latin tongue," he complained to the boy, Francesco, who was his chum in the school to which he was sent in Florence as soon as he was old enough, "though that is not what I want to know most, nor do I want to learn a trade like my brothers. Nor do I want to become a learned scholar, no, not even to please my father."

"Say no more," laughed Francesco; "I am not blind to all the drawings you have been making day in and day out whether you learned a Latin word or not. Neither am I deaf to the wishes you have sighed for so many times. You want to go with me to the workshop of my master, the great Domenico Ghirlandajo, who paints so well that he has mightily pleased the great Medici duke. Beg your father to let you study there with me!"

"Let it be so," at length sighed Lodovico, Michelangelo's father. "I can neither persuade nor force him to learn a trade or become a man of letters, such a noble calling. He thinks and talks of nothing but drawing and painting and carving. 'Tis as if he drew in that desire with each breath of the clear air on the hillsides near the stone quarries where he was nursed as an infant. Let him try his wings. Mayhap he will come flying back to me! I will, forthwith, apprentice him to this Ghirlandajo, the painter in Florence. Although I don't think so much of these arts of painting and carving."

"Ah, but the Magnificent does!" answered the friend to whom Lodovico had been confiding his misgivings. "He is always looking for someone who can build, or paint, or carve in such an excellent manner that he adds beauty and fame to our city. Just as he is always befriending those who write well and make excellent music. Wait, Lodovico, you may be very proud of your boy yet!"

There was a great deal for a thirteen-year-old boy to do and to learn in the artist's workshop. It was encouraging to all the apprentice boys to know that the master himself had not always been a painter of pictures. Ghirlandajo had at first followed in his father's footsteps and studied under him the goldsmith's art. Why, his very name meant "maker of garlands," a name given his father because he could make for the ladies of Florence such wonderful garlands of silver and gold. Domenico's skilful fingers, too, learned to twist the fine gold wire and beat out his patterns of flowers and leaves in gold and in silver. But the goldsmith's art did not satisfy him and he began to try his hand at painting pictures, portraits of the folk of Florence, until he became a great favorite with all those, great and small, who wished to live upon canvas during the centuries to come.

Michelangelo became so skilful with his pen, his pencil and his brush, that he soon surpassed all the other apprentice boys and often astounded the master himself.

"I would know that the master had once been a goldsmith," Michelangelo confided to Francesco, who always worked by his side whenever he could. "See! there in the portraits of those grand ladies, the patterns upon their brocaded robes and their golden ornaments. Almost as real as if they were made of gold and of silver. Come, let us go and watch him at work upon his wall paintings in the church of Santa Maria Novella."

" 'Tis said that right in the midst of the Holy Pictures he is painting for the two noble families of Florence who want to do honor to their names, there are portraits of them," observed Francesco.

"Fine portraits they are, too," declared the boy Michelangelo, who would soon equal and surpass his master. "Though I could wish that he paid less heed to the decorations on their robes, and more to the inner likenesses of the people themselves."

Michelangelo soon grew weary in Ghirlandajo's workshop and felt that he would like to try his hand at something all by himself. He had learned all he could in watching the master paint his pictures on the walls of the chapel in the church of Santa Maria Novella; he had even helped whenever the master was willing. But he did long to work out for himself the ideas which so vividly came to his mind.

"I know what we shall do, my impatient Michelangelo," declared Francesco enthusiastically. "We will go to some beautiful gardens I know about: the gardens of San Marco, which belong to Lorenzo the Magnificent. There are all sorts of statues gleaming amidst the green, carved, some of them, by sculptors hundreds and hundreds of years ago. There you shall draw what you will."

"My Francesco," declared Michelangelo, making ready to go at once, "my fingers not only can make pictures in line and color, but model them in the round. Was I not nursed as a babe by a stonecutter's daughter, hearing the sound of chisels and hammers each day in the great stone quarries? Why, 'tis in the very blood and heart of me!

"This is a true school of art," cried the delighted boy, Michelangelo, "far better than staying day after day in one workshop. I am coming here to study and work every day that the master will spare me."

"We are honored!" Francesco ran into the inner workshop to tell his chum, Michelangelo, one early spring morning. "The Magnificent is in the outer shop talking to the master! Truly, he is good to look upon, though he is rather dark and squints his eyes as if he could not see very far. But he has a friendly smile, and his voice, though harsh, falls pleasantly upon the ear. Let us peer in through that partly open door!"

They nearly gave themselves away when they heard the Medici duke say, "I have come to take your most promising pupils, my Domenico, to place them in my gardens among the beautiful statues there, and see what they can do. Which of those who learn from your skill will you send to me?"

"My most promising pupil, Excellency, though not the most gracious because of his impetuous desire to go ahead by himself, is Michelangelo Buonarroti; and Francesco Granacci is very careful in detail though not so powerful in line or original in thought. They shall go, Magnificence."

"Oh, Francesco," breathed Michelangelo, as they tiptoed back to the inner shop. "Think of it, every day to work by ourselves in those beautiful gardens! All praise to Lorenzo the Magnificent!"

"And all thanks to the master for choosing us," added the gentler Francesco.

The sun mellowed the marbles in those beautiful gardens, the air was sweet with the flowers, and Michelangelo was happy. "Observe, my Francesco, this head of an old Faun! see how the old fellow grins! I shall try my hand at carving him, especially his widely curving mouth. How good it seems to be carving instead of handling the pen or pencil, yea, even colors."

"Aha!" he later heard a voice say close to his ear. "So you have chosen this old Faun. It is well done and your master, Ghirlandajo, will be pleased with the skill you have shown. Yet, though you have made the grinning fellow the possessor of many years, you have not taken away from him a single tooth! Do you not know that one or two are always missing when men grow to that great age?"

Michelangelo was quite overwhelmed at first to have His Excellency, Duke Lorenzo, address him. But the Duke's smile quite reassured him. Quickly Michelangelo knocked out a tooth!

"You are quick to act," laughed the great Lorenzo, "and show promise for the future. Go, now, to your father, and ask him to come to me, for I would speak with him."

"Nay," complained his father, decidedly shaking his head, "His Magnificence will lead you astray, boy that you are. I will have no stonecutter for a son."

"Nay, Father," explained the impatient Michelangelo. "A sculptor is quite different from a stonecutter. I shall add beauty to the city of Florence and honor to you!"

So Lodovico was persuaded to present himself before Duke Lorenzo. "Your son has great talent, yea, genius, Lodovico. I can help him and he can serve Florence. We have need of such as he is, for genius is all too rare. Will you not let me take him within my palace under my protection and see that he has every help in his art?"

At first Lodovico was silent; but the Magnificent had such a winning way of talking, that it was hard to refuse him. Besides, he was the great Medici duke!

"My son, Michelangelo, and each one of us are at the pleasure of your Magnificence," he finally said.

The boy felt almost as if he were living in a dream, as day after day he enjoyed his life in the Medici palace. There was so much to see and so much to learn. Vases, statues by the great masters, beautiful manuscript pages most delicately written by hand, paintings by his old master and others who had helped to beautify Florence. Such wonderful people were guests in the palace halls! Michelangelo had heard of many of them; who in Florence had not? Poets whose very words were like music; musicians who filled the palace halls with a harmony of sound which made him dream and plan of the beauty his fingers would produce; philosophers and scholars who dug at the roots of all things; the great religious teacher, Savonarola, who preached to the people of Florence. Michelangelo grew to know them all, for he was treated by Duke Lorenzo as one of his own sons.

"I must work hard," Michelangelo would promise himself, "and study daily from the works of the Greeks and the Romans, who understood the human form so well;

and from Nature, who was their great teacher as surely as she is mine. Yet must I follow my own dreams, for only so can I make the Magnificent and our City of Flowers, for which he has done so much, proud of me. I can learn much from the paintings of the noble Masaccio on the walls of the chapel he has painted."

There one day he got into trouble; he could draw so well that his comrades were rather envious of his skill. "He thinks he is better than the rest of us!" cried Piero Torrigiano, one of the boys who was most envious. "Just because he lives in the house of the Medici!"

"Ha!" retorted Michelangelo, fingers busy as he easily copied one of the most difficult figures. "If you would work a little harder you would have less grumbling to offend the ears!"

Piero's face grew red with anger. His arm shot out and his clenched fist gave poor Michelangelo's unsuspecting nose such a violent blow that it was broken at the bridge!

Yet, despite some differences with his fellow-students, partly because he was so far beyond them in his work, those days in the household of the Medici family were very happy ones. Gay and joyous they often were with the pageants which the Duke prepared to the delight of the people of Florence. Michelangelo's friend, Francesco, had a great deal to do with planning the processions, the music, the dances; and the artists of Florence did their part in adorning the banners, the shields, and the chariots. Michelangelo did his share, for he could write verses as well as paint and carve. In the midst of the gay festivals, the processions with the blare of trumpets, the bright colors, the shining armor and painted banners, the dancing and the songs bidding everyone to enjoy each day since they knew not what might happen on the morrow, Lorenzo the Magnificent died, and Michelangelo lost his very good friend. Lorenzo's son was not great enough or strong enough to take his father's place in Florence, and much trouble followed.

Michelangelo went to Venice, then to Bologna, where he and the two friends who traveled with him were cast into prison! "A warm reception," they muttered ruefully, "just because we did not know that every foreigner entering the gates must be marked on the thumb with a seal of red wax!" Luckily for them, a nobleman paid their fines on hearing that Michelangelo was a sculptor, and kept him as a guest for more than a year. But again, artists of Bologna who were not so gifted as he, were envious, and threatened to do him mischief if he stayed any longer taking to himself orders for work which belonged to them.

So back again he went to his beloved city of Florence very much changed from the days when the great Lorenzo who loved gayety, color, and beauty, was the leader. There were still great artists there: his old master, Ghirlandajo, the marvelous Leonardo who was a genius in so many things, and a young man named Raphael, who one day would do even greater things, so the older folks prophesied. One of the statues which Michelangelo carved at that time won him fame in Rome, which city he had always wanted to visit.

Near the great Cathedral of Flowers in Florence, from which he could not stay away very long, was a huge block of marble which no artist had been able to turn into a beautiful statue. Even the wonderful Leonardo had decided that he could not make anything out of it.

"Let this Michelangelo try his hand at it," advised one of the Florentines who wanted to see something made from that huge marble block. "If anyone can do anything with it, he can. He is a giant himself in thought and in work. His praises are being sung in Rome because of the

Sleeping Cupid which he carved and which, unsigned, he sent to Rome. It was so beautifully done that it was sold as an old statue dug up from the Roman times. The cardinal who bought it at last suspected that a fine modern artist had carved it, and sent one of his men to Florence to find him. He visited our Michelangelo, watched him draw one of his perfect hands which no other sculptor can equal, heard him tell about a cupid he had once carved, and knew he had found the right artist. To Rome he was taken, to the palace of the cardinal, who at once gave him orders for work. He is the man to make something out of this marble—something worthy of Florence."

Under Michelangelo's magic fingers the block of marble was changed into the beautiful statue of David, the shepherd boy, his slingshot over his shoulder, ready to go forth, alone, to overcome a giant.

How he did work! chiseling, pounding, creating, until he had freed the figure of the shepherd boy which he felt was imprisoned within, only waiting for the thoughts of his mind and the blows of his chisel to free it.

"Hail to our Michelangelo!" cried the delighted people of Florence. "His statue seems to breathe, to be about to move, to whirl the stone into the air against his enemy, the Giant Goliath! Such a lifelike, wonderful hand, marble turned into flesh."

The next year Pope Julius II called Michelangelo to Rome to carve for him a magnificent tomb to be erected in the old Church of Saint Peter. Michelangelo selected great blocks of the finest marble, and eagerly went to work. But alas! some interfering folk told the Pope that it was an evil omen to build his tomb in his lifetime, and he stopped Michelangelo's work for some time. The Pope decided that he wanted Michelangelo to cover with pictures the ceiling of the Sistine Chapel of the Vatican, close to that very Church of Saint Peter which he was later to crown with a glorious dome.

"Nay, Your Holiness," pleaded Michelangelo, "I am a sculptor at heart, not a painter. Give this honor to Raphael, who understands all about color. I should never be able to please you in painting these pictures!"

"Thou wilt suit me quite well," answered the Pope very decidedly. "Thou art the one I have chosen. Color training thou hast had in Florence with Domenico Ghirlandajo. Come! the scaffolding is already being erected. Once thou makest up thy mind to it, there is nothing thou canst not do, so great an artist thou art. Paint for me the Bible story of the creation of the earth and of man, the entrance of sin into the world, and the flood."

"If I must paint this gigantic picture book for His Holiness, then I must," Michelangelo decided. "But I shall paint it in my own way, and the beauty and design of the human body, the greatest work of God, shall always be my chief concern."

Day after day the great picture book grew with its wonderful figures of men and women and children, painted as Michelangelo the sculptor would carve, so that they seemed almost in the round, in colors of orange and bronze, russets, lilacs, cool greens and blues.

"So weary I get lying upon my back, looking upward," sighed Michelangelo after days and weeks and many months had passed. "Pains shoot through my head, my neck, and my eyes. In truth I am getting so that I cannot read except when I am lying upon my back and holding my paper up over my head!" And at night after many hours of constant work, sometimes with only a piece of bread to eat at noon so intent was he upon what he was doing, he went wearily home to his lonely house to work some more —planning and sketching the figures he hoped to complete the next day, sometimes working during the night.

Pope Julius impatiently watched his great picture book grow.

"When shall I be able to show these holy pictures to the people of Rome?" he asked one day, unable to wait any longer.

"Patience, Your Holiness," begged Michelangelo, looking down upon him from where he was lying upon the high scaffolding. "I shall finish the figures—and there are many of them, Your Holiness—just as soon as I am able. I want to make them as beautiful as I can."

"Nay, thou shalt finish them now!" answered the Pope, losing his temper. "Else I shall be tempted to hurl thee from the scaffolding!"

"That thou shalt never do," Michelangelo said to himself. "I will leave them as they are!"

It was a great day in Rome when the people gathered to see the gigantic picture book. "It is magnificent, overwhelming!" they murmured. "Think of Michelangelo's genius in creating those beautiful, powerful forms, looking almost as if they were modeled; his endurance in painting while lying upon his back! Even our great painter, Raphael, is impressed." " 'Tis a masterpiece, a gigantic picture book," all agreed. "Michelangelo is a master artist and his mighty works shall last always to the wonder and awe of all men."

RAPHAEL

1483–1520

BEFORE THE STORY

THE LIFE of Raffaello Santi, whom we know as Raphael, seems too wonderful to be true. And yet we know that it is, since true accounts have come down to us.

In the story we will visit the boy Raphael in his home in Urbino, just about the very year when a fellow countryman, Cristofero Colombo, or Christopher Columbus, as we call him, had gained the help he had long sought to find new lands to the westward. To Perugia, Florence, and Rome we will go with him after his dream of becoming a painter had come true.

So beautiful are the pictures he has left us, each with its message of peace, of religious feeling, of beauty, that we forget the artist who painted them and think only of the smiling landscapes, the gentle, loving mothers and fair, chubby babies, saints and angels and cherubs he has left us. Many of them were completed in a very short time, for Raphael lived only thirty-seven years.

Raphael had for a teacher Pietro Perugino whose gracious, lovely landscapes are often reflected in those of his pupil. He knew the Magician Painter, Leonardo, and that Giant of Artists, Michelangelo. He marveled at their work and learned from them. They, in turn, felt that the young Raphael would become one of the greatest of painters. Everyone liked Raphael, even his rivals, so great was his grace and charm.

Raphael had for a friend the religious painter, Fra

Bartolomeo, a follower of the teachings of that powerful religious teacher, Savonarola, who stirred all Florence. They, too, bore influence upon his works, and no doubt helped towards the creation of those most beautiful of pictures, beautiful in every sense of the word, of the Holy Mother and Child.

Though Raphael worked for many great dignitaries of the church and state, yet he always remained simple and sincere, generous and helpful always to his friends. Like the good Saint Francis, his fellow countryman, who also lived among the Umbrian hills, he loved mankind and wanted to add to the good in the world.

When he was only twenty-five he went to Rome to paint for the same Pope Julius the Second for whom the great Michelangelo painted the Story of the Creation of the Earth on the ceiling of the Sistine Chapel. Raphael caught the likeness of the Pope upon his canvas and made him live through the ages. He has made us see him an old man, yet full of many thoughts, plans of great works, and the will to see them completed. He gave to the portrait richness of color, a deep red cap, red violet cape, and white vestment vibrating with light.

For Pope Julius it was that Raphael began, and for Pope Leo the Tenth finished, those wonderful wall paintings in the Vatican Palace in Rome, so perfect in design, and in color, so lofty and grand in space.

For King Francis the First of France, a lover of beauty whom the great Leonardo also served, Raphael painted the young Saint Michael, conqueror over the Evil One.

Of all Raphael's pictures of the Holy Mother and Child, perhaps we know best "The Sistine Madonna" and "The Madonna of the Chair." The former shows the Holy Mother and Child with Saints Barbara and Sixtus and is known and loved the world over. In this picture he has shown us a Heavenly Mother and Child, in a beautiful triangular space. It is full of grace, dramatic in line, in grouping, and in gesture, each color in true harmony with its neighbor. Some adorable little cherubs peer out at us. The latter shows the loving, human mother with her plump bambino (baby) held close to her, and the little Saint John also helps draw our attention to them. Just follow, in the illustration included in this book, the curve of the line from the mother's head to her baby held so close to her; or the straight line of the chair arm which points to the mother where her curved arm again leads us to the baby the artist most wants us to see. Line harmonizes with line, color with color, not one out of scale or out of place. And surely the forms look real—the baby so plump, so chubby, soft flesh yielding to the touch, so full of life. Most truly has Raphael often been called the Prince of Painters.

Some of Raphael's Paintings:

THE SCHOOL OF ATHENS (*mural*)
Vatican, Rome
MADONNA DEL GRANDUCA
Pitti Gallery, Florence
PORTRAIT OF POPE JULIUS THE SECOND
Pitti Gallery, Florence
LA BELLE JARDINIÈRE
Louvre, Paris
THE COLONNA MADONNA
Metropolitan Museum of Art, New York

ALBA MADONNA
National Gallery of Art, Washington
PORTRAIT OF BINDO ALTOVITI
National Gallery of Art, Washington
COUNT TOMMASO INGHIRAMI
Isabella Stewart Gardner Museum, Boston

A BOY ARTIST OF URBINO: RAFFAELLO SANTI

Urbino, the home of illustrious dukes, was a very good place in which to be born, with its grand palace, its craggy mountains, its green plains and valleys and woodlands. A rugged and somber beauty, it is true, yet quiet and peaceful. In Urbino it was, in Umbria, that Raffaello Santi was born on Good Friday night, and the stars in the purple sky must have been propitious and the Saints and Angels beyond must have smiled down upon him and showered him with gifts.

Giovanni Santi, Raffaello's father, was an upstanding man in Urbino, and one who loved his trade, that of a painter, though never did he win in it the success he desired.

"Magia *cara*," he would earnestly say to the baby's mother, "we must take great care in the rearing of our boy. Two have we lost, may God pity us, and now Raffaello has come to comfort us. We must give him such training and learning that he will do honor to the name of Santi, and bring glory to the great Archangel for whom he is named."

"Thou art right, Giovanni *mio*," nodded the mother. "Our boy shall never be given to a nurse to bring up; we will care for him and train him and be made thrice happy thereby."

Raphael was very happy in his home and adored his parents, who watched over him so tenderly. He was happy in the beauties he saw around him, for his eyes, even when he was very small, were quick to see beauty.

"The mountains stretch up to the pretty blue sky," he would confide to his mother, "and the plains go miles and miles away to big cities. The sea, ever sparkling and changing, ripples out to meet the sky—and we in Urbino are up so high in the Apennine hills that we can see it all, just as far as the eye can reach! Make a picture of it, my father, as we see it now!"

Giovanni Santi smiled and sighed and shook his head. Had he not been making many pictures without ever reaching success?

"I shall try it one day," the small Raphael thought as he watched his father at work. "There will be much to choose from: hills and fields and high rocky cliffs with the castle of the great dukes upon them. Duke Guidobaldo loves beauty too, as his father, Duke Frederick, did, for always he has artists and poets in his castle, to encourage them in their work. Perhaps one day he will help me, and let me have a peep at the books in his library I've heard tell about and at the pictures painted by great masters upon his castle walls.

"Has not the Duchess Elizabeth asked my father to paint for her a portrait of her own fair self? And has he not written in rhyming words all about the brave deeds of Duke Guidobaldo's father? The Duchess Elizabeth showed it to me one day when I was there to see the fine paintings and carvings. I, too, would make something of beauty!"

"Help me all thou wilt, my Raffaello," Giovanni Santi

would encourage him. "See, Magia, look at him, our boy, is he not young to know the meaning of lines and to have such an aptitude for color?"

So day after day the dark-eyed, fair-haired boy, Raphael, grew wiser in the teachings his mother and father gave him. Day after day he drank in all of the beauty he could find. The sunlight upon water or the spear-tips of soldiers, waving fields of grain, shadowy crags, the green of valleys and the soft colors of blossoming trees all appealed to him. Day after day he listened to the music of the church bells, and followed his father and mother to prayer. Often the pictures he saw in the little church and in the high, strong-walled castle by masters of Italy and Flanders, made him hope that one day he, too, might tell holy stories by means of his pictures.

There was a court in the big castle where tournaments were held, so often the boy's thoughts were turned towards knights in shining armor who tilted with long lances while banners waved, and plumes danced from the heads of the prancing horses. The clear mountain air was filled many a time with the cheers of the Duke's retainers and the tinkle of laughter from the jeweled ladies.

Sometimes he thought aloud to his good friend, Timoteo Viti, who had painted pictures of the angels for the Grand Duke's palace and for the Holy Church, and who with Raffaello's father, was teaching him how to hold the pencil and the brush and to make line and color obey his desire. "Master Timoteo, when I look at those shining knights in armor, I think of Saint George, who with his bright sword freed the fair Princess from the Dragon, or of Saint Michael, who likewise overcame the Evil One. One day, good Timoteo, I shall picture them—or a knight just about to start out on his quest—one day you shall see!"

"Bah! away with all this learning and grinding and mixing of colors!" came the harsh voice of Bernadina, the stepmother who had come to the Santi home after the loss of Raphael's own, beautiful mother. "It is nonsense! Let the boy learn a trade which will bring us some money. This painting business brings in little enough, Giovanni, judging by you and your fine friend Timoteo, whom Raphael is forever following."

Raphael could no more have changed his beauty-loving nature than could his father or teacher, but he kept from his stepmother's sight as much as he could. His very appearance as well as his habits were enough to throw her into a fit of anger. "Dreamer! Good-for-nothing!" she would mutter. "Just like his daydreaming father!"

"Oh, Timoteo," grieved Raphael, three years later. "How can I bear it? How can I live without my father to help me and love me and teach me? It was bad enough with my dear mother gone, but now, with my father gone, the light has gone from the sun, the blue from the sky, and the melody from the birds' songs. There is no beauty, no peace in our home, just unkind words and sharp quarrels over my dear father's money!"

"Comfort thyself, Raffaello," begged the kind Timoteo. "Comfort thyself with the thought that thy father would wish thee to take up his work where he left it and carry it on better than he, and give of the best in thee, and through thee in him, that more beauty may be given the world."

Try as hard as he could, Raphael could no longer exclaim with delight at the jousts between skilful knights in the courtyard of the Duke's palace; at the Ducal party riding swiftly away to the hunt, their horses galloping, horns sounding, dogs baying. Only was he happy when he caught a glimpse of a golden dish made by a master goldsmith, or a delicately carved ivory box brought by a pilgrim from an Eastern land, or a colorful bowl fashioned by the fine potters of Urbino, their art high in the Duke's favor.

It comforted him to watch the master potters shaping the jars and the bowls from the finest of clay, baking them in the hottest of fires, painting designs and landscapes upon them, giving them an enamel bath which the fire changed to rich, glowing, lustrous colors. The master potters were giving of their best to increase the beauty in Urbino and the outer world, and more and more often the Duke sent them an order for a jar, a basin, or a platter with pictures painted upon them in the most beautiful enameled colors, to grace his castle or to be sent as a gift to a neighboring duke or prince. For the art of pottery making was taking a high place among the other arts of the day.

Still Raphael was restless and could not settle down to his work again in Urbino. He went to Perugia, boy though he was, to study in the workshop of the great Pietro Vanucci, far better known as Perugino.

"Will he take a fifteen-year-old boy, nearly sixteen, for his pupil, think you, good Timoteo?" asked Raphael, all anxiety as he was about to start out. "My dear father always wanted me to go to the great Perugino's workshop."

"When he sees what you can do, my Raffaello," cheered the artist Timoteo Viti, who had given him what training he could, "we shall all be proud of you. That, I predict."

As Raphael, in company with an uncle, his mother's brother who was guardian over him, drew near his new home, dreams once again filled his heart and his mind and were mirrored in his eyes, and the old desire came back to make those dreams come true. Again and again he drank from the beauty of the Perugia he was nearing.

"How softly blue are the gently sloping hills with their olive trees," he murmured, "so different from the steep, rugged ones of Urbino. Veil-draped they seem to be as the mists cover them. Ah, there are the battlements which have grown from those of old Roman walls. Yes, I feel I shall be happy here," and he smiled again at the beauty of the countryside where he was to make his new home.

Raphael's heart was in his mouth as he stood in Perugino's workshop which looked to him so big and filled with so many pupils.

"Wilt thou take him, Messere?" asked the good uncle, anxiously. "His father was a painter of Urbino and taught him when he was a small lad, and Master Timoteo Viti likewise of Urbino has trained him well. Giovanni Santi, the boy's father—may the good God bless him and rest him in peace—was anxious for him to come to thee."

Raphael said not a word, but stood before Perugino, straight, slender, his dark dream-filled eyes beneath his light hair pleading for him.

Pietro Perugino looked long at the drawings the boy had made. "Gladly will I take thee, Raffaello," he answered in his gentle, courteous manner. "Always I have room for a pupil who shows promise, and thou dost show great promise of creating beauty with thy hands. Perugia, the battleground of rival families, is now at peace and the thoughts of all who love her are turned towards her beautifying. Buildings must be restored, walls decorated, panels painted for the Church Fathers. Come, Raffaello, thou art welcome, for I can see from thy face as well as from thy drawings, that thou wilt give peace and beauty to thy pictures. In the future I see thee a great painter beloved by Italy and one day my master."

"Persevere in all things," Perugino instructed his pupils. "Let not cold nor hunger nor discouragement keep you from perfecting your God-given gifts. The sun will not always shine, but after the clouds comes clear sunny weather. And remember to take pains in little things. Above all, take good care to perfect your drawing, as the good goldsmith-painter of Florence, Verrocchio, taught me. Lay your foundation well in that, and the understanding of light and shadow, and of color will follow. Always make sketches each day of that which brings you interest."

Raphael obeyed him well and, sketch book under his arm, drew the folk of Perugia, the public buildings, and especially the blue-veiled hills and silver-hued olive trees, and painted them gentle and soft in coloring.

The Master was quick to see the good work his favorite pupil did, and soon asked for his help with religious pictures, for so apt a follower Raphael had been that it was often hard to know which figures were from the brush of the Master.

Still Raphael dreamed and sketched, though sometimes he longed to see other cities. When Perugino went to Florence, he longed to follow the master whom he loved to that City of Flowers where dreams came true, ambition filled the clear air, and where there were great leaders eager to encourage young artists that Florence might be the most beautiful city of Italy. When one of his fellow pupils in Perugino's workshop went to Siena to adorn the walls of the Cathedral Library, Raphael gladly followed when he sent for him to help, for there he would see new sights, make new friends, and besides, Siena was much nearer the wonder city of Florence.

"I must go to Florence," he often confided to his friend, Pinturicchio. "There are artists there whose work I must see, especially Leonardo, who also came from a hilltop village. He has done such wonderful work that he is already an honored member of the famous Guild of Florentine Painters—and he only twenty! Then, there is the mighty Michelangelo, that giant of sculptors who has cut the hero David from a great block of marble which no one could make use of before. To Florence I must go, and from those artists I must learn."

Always willing to learn from others, Raphael stood in wonder before the works of these two great artists, and little by little caught the new spirit in art which they breathed, and made it his own. The very same Pope, Julius, who asked or rather commanded Michelangelo to paint the ceiling of his chapel in the Vatican Palace in Rome, asked Raphael to come to Rome to decorate certain rooms in that palace. "I hope that my father knows," thought Raphael; "I hope that he knows my dreams I had as a boy, dreams which he shared, are really coming true."

Different from those lofty, wonderful pictures which he painted upon the walls of the Pope's palace, but far more enjoyed by everyday folk, are his mothers and children, such loving, tender mothers and such chubby, curly-headed babies, so real and lifelike, painted with understanding, beauty of line, of form and of color.

"Paint for me a Holy Mother and Baby, simple, real, beautiful, like the mother love we can see any day here in our city of Florence, my Raffaello," urged a member of that famous Medici family who encouraged the artists, writers, poets, musicians of the day. "Make it appeal to all mothers—throughout our land." This is the story which has grown up about that picture which Raphael painted in answer to his request.

Up among the shadowed, mist-bathed hills surrounding Florence, long before the time of Raphael, there lived an old hermit named Bernardo. In his little cottage he enjoyed each calm and quiet and peaceful day, happy in the beauties of Nature around him, in the comfort of his religious thoughts. Gentle showers watered the vineyards but the sun soon shone again. One day black clouds piled up on the hilltops and rolled over them in great dark and threatening masses. Thunder shook the hills and the echoes went roaring on and on like the deepest of church music, so the good Bernardo thought. But when the lightnings flashed in great forked streams so that the very sky seemed to open and rain fire upon the hills and even into the valleys, then Bernardo trembled, though he said his prayers and felt comforted.

Mighty winds shrieked and howled and tore at the trees of the vineyards, and when they were calmed down, over the hillsides roared and tumbled the loosened waters, sweeping all before them, uprooting great trees, setting strong houses afloat, a storm the like of which had never before swept the hillside.

Bernardo felt the water rising and tried to reach the high branches of a strong oak tree which had withstood the wind's blasts. But Bernardo was old and lame and could not swing himself up from the ground.

"Reach yonder branch as I lift, good Father," he heard a voice gasp, as Mary, the beautiful young daughter of the master of the vineyard, helped him reach safety in the staunch old tree.

"Holy One, who has now stilled the raging storm," prayed Bernardo that night, "may there be some way in thy mercy that in the years to come the memory of this maiden and of the oak tree, my saviors, may be kept."

Years passed by, and Mary still worked hard in the vineyards which yielded well. That one bad storm of the countryside was almost forgotten. There was so much to do that there was little time for dreaming, for Mary had two plump baby boys. The sturdy old oak was cut down and sawed into timber which was used for making casks.

One sunny, summer day, Mary sat in the courtyard of her hillside house near the newly made casks, playing with her happy dimpled boys. "Come, *carissimo!*" she laughed and caught one of them to her arms and held him close. "And come thou, *mio caro,*" she called to the other boy, old enough to trudge away to find treasures of his own. "Show Mother Mary what thou hast found!" Laughing merrily, he came running to her side, in his chubby hands two little sticks which he held together in the shape of a cross.

A stranger from the city, judging by his rich tunic and his velvet cape, passed by. Hearing the happy laughter he peered within, and feasted his eyes upon the group with their soft colors of blue, rose, green, and golden brown, warmed by the sun.

"What I have long sought!" he murmured, as with a smile and bow, and a hushing of the mother's protest by his raised hand, he looked around for something upon which to sketch them before the pose was lost. His sketch book was filled to its very last leaf. With a bit of charcoal from the hearth of the courtyard, he swiftly drew upon the head of a wine cask, made from that sturdy oak tree, the gentle mother and her plump bambinos, one held tenderly in her arms, the other pressed close to her side. And from that swift sketch, the painter, the great Raphael of Urbino, Perugia, and the mighty cities of Florence and of Rome, the Prince of Painters, made the picture which the whole world loves, the Mother of the Chair. Thus the memory of Mary and the sturdy oak tree are kept forever, as the old hermit prayed. It was captured by the skill of Raphael, the painter of Italy known and loved everywhere even after these hundreds of years.

EL GRECO

c. 1545–*c.* 1614

BEFORE THE STORY

A VERY great painter of Spain had a very long name—Domenicos Theotocopoulos—a Greek name hard to manage! We don't wonder that he was nicknamed "El Greco—The Greek." As so often happens, nicknames are remembered even when the real names are forgotten, so this Spanish painter is best known today by his nickname, "El Greco."

About four hundred years ago he was born on the island of Crete, which had such a wonderful art of its own long before the Greek art on the mainland. It was in Crete that treasure seekers found the long-sought-for home of the later Greek civilization. It was there that they found the many-roomed palace of King Minos, his throne-chair, his jars for the storing of grain, so huge that they might well have hidden Ali Baba's forty thieves! Golden cups with pictures of bulls beaten out upon them were discovered; dagger blades with gold engraved bull-hunting scenes from Candia, Crete, the town where El Greco lived; vases with carved figures of winnowers, their winnowing forks over their shoulders, marching along to the rhythm of the song they seemed to be singing; vases with painted patterns of waves and fish, shells and ships.

King Minos, Ruler of the Waves, had many ships and traded with many lands. Upon the walls of his palace, over thirty-five hundred years old yet almost modern with its fine drainage system, were found bright-colored paintings of Cretan men and women in the fashionable dress of the court, and what is often called the "Cretan Circus," a scene showing boy and girl toreadors skilfully meeting a very fierce bull, perhaps the Minotaur which Theseus, the Greek hero from the mainland, overcame.

At any rate, part of the well-known story has been proved to be true by these treasure seekers. There was a King Minos who lived in a wonderful palace, who had a princess daughter named Ariadne, and who encouraged bullfighting at his court, and bullhunting in the marshes! The treasures discovered show remarkable art both painted and carved, and a goldsmith's art, wonderful indeed. All figures are full of life and color and the artists were eager for expression in many ways.

So small Domenicos, or El Greco as we will call him, lived as a boy on this very remarkable island where artists, thousands of years before, enriched the art of the people of the mainland, the Greeks as we know them, who in turn, still several thousand years ago, produced such perfection and beauty that artists from that time on have always learned from them.

El Greco early went to Venice and learned a great deal from the skill of the famous Titian, whose pupil he became when he was about twenty years old. But he learned most of all from Tintoretto, whose religious pictures gave him many ideas for his own. Yet El Greco, because of the very strength of his personality, has always stood very much alone. He painted not only what he saw with his physical eyes but with the eyes of his mind as well. He combined the real things around him with original ideas of his own. Strange though his figures may seem with their long, thin forms and faces, there is always the rhythm of line, the feeling of movement, the happy effect one color has upon another.

Among the illustrations in this book is El Greco's "View of Toledo."

Is not the picture a strange, poetical, yet real and sincere rendering of Toledo? Imagine it in color with its cold greens and blues, its cloud-swept sky, its flashes of light, its dramatic glimpse of a violent storm just about to break! Color plays an important part in giving us the effect. Toledo in Spain was a city to which El Greco most truly belonged.

His religious pictures are poetical, too, full of deep religious feeling, though at first the strangeness in the proportions of the figures affects us. His portraits show the power to reveal the spirit as well as the form.

Some of El Greco's Pictures:

PORTRAIT OF GIULIO CLOVIO
National Museum, Naples

HOLY FAMILY
Prado Museum, Madrid

ADORATION OF THE SHEPHERDS
Church of Santo Domingo el Antigua, Toledo

CARDINAL DON FERNANDO NIÑO DE GUEVARA
Metropolitan Museum of Art, New York

THE NATIVITY
Metropolitan Museum of Art, New York

ST. MARTIN AND THE BEGGAR
National Gallery of Art, Washington

HOLY FAMILY
Hispanic Society of America, New York

THE REPENTANT PETER
Phillips Memorial Gallery, Washington

HOLY FAMILY
Museum of Art, Cleveland, Ohio
FRAY FELIZ HORTENSIO PALLAVICINO
Museum of Fine Arts, Boston

EL GRECO: PAINTER OF SPAIN

"Domenicos Theotocopoulos! What a mouthful, lad! El Greco, 'the Greek,' is surely far easier to manage," laughed Jacopo Robusti, known throughout Italy as Tintoretto, "the little dyer," a name given him because of his father's trade.

The slender, pale-faced Greek boy smiled with his lips but his great, dark eyes kept their somberness.

"It means—my name, oh, Messere Tintoretto—'the little Son of God,' or the 'Bird of God.' "

"And a beautiful name it is, lad, and good use you have made of it in the few years you've been picturemaking with old Bassano, so called from the place in which he lives high up among the mountains. Jacopo da Ponte he was christened. Rumors have come even to Venice from the master who trained you and used you and tried to make your work a copy of his own. Make the Greek a Venetian? Out upon such stupidity! Just a look at your pale, slender face, boy, and one will know that you'll always be yourself, 'The Greek,' in whose pictures line follows line in strange rhythm, and color blends with color. Color, lad, is something you have from Crete and I from Venice. Shall I ever get the blue of the Adriatic right, here in this picture, as background for the Doge in Prayer before the Redeemer? You, with your love for color, shall tell me just what you think of it."

El Greco followed Tintoretto's eyes to the blue and gold of the Grand Canal which flowed beneath them as they stood upon the Rialto bridge. He looked beyond to the deeper blue of the sea of which Venice had long been the proud Queen. The gondolas, as they glided, were gently disturbing the reflections in the water. Farther out upon the deeper blue, yet still with dancing golden lights, were high-hulled ships, the white crests of waves breaking against their sides, bright sails filling. To the boy, Domenicos, they looked like "Birds of God."

"It's a deeper blue now, Master Tintoretto, out there where the breeze is beginning to ripple the waters, and the sails snap in the wind. Ah, now you have it upon your canvas! Oh, Master Tintoretto, so lovely and deep and clear a color it is that folk will look at that and the brown hulls of those Venetian ships, the background of your picture, rather than upon the kneeling doge and the Redeemer!"

Tintoretto laughed. "Let them if they wish, boy. Without that color, the beauty of my picture would be lost. With it, the religious message is just the same—for seeing eyes. Tell me now, El Greco, or Domenicos, whatever you want me to call you, how do you like your Titian's workshop? I was his pupil, too, remember. Titian is now an old man. How do you like him and his shop?"

Domenicos hesitated, uncertain just what to say, for he had heard more times than one since he had reached Venice that through jealousy Titian had sent away his gifted pupil, this very Tintoretto. But that was as it might be. Titian was a great painter, the pride of Venice, and there was no one like him.

"I have learned in Titian's workshop a great deal in the laying on of colors, in the skilful holding of my brush. Most of all I have learned by watching him paint so swiftly. Never will I forget the first day that I went there!"

Tintoretto looked up expectantly from the blue of the Adriatic he was painting with the proud ships upon it, always to tell the story that Venice was the Mistress of the Seas.

"Titian, the immortal, lives in the midst of beauty, Messere, does he not? Beautiful gardens leading to a beautiful house, and in that house such treasures! Gold and silver and jewels are there, tapestries upon the walls, and wonderful sculpture made by artists of my land. I tell you, Messere Tintoretto, as I looked upon them I was proud that I am a Greek! Such beautifully carved ceilings shining with gold there were, too, and such wonderful canvases upon which he and his pupils were working. Ah, Messere, at last I was about to be taught by a great painter! You, too, are great, oh, Tintoretto," added El Greco hastily, fearing that he had offended. "Do they not say in Venice that Titian feared the genius of his young pupil?"

"They say this and they say that in Venice, El Greco, they of the wagging tongues. It is not for us now to judge the greatest painter Venice will ever know. Though Titian did not keep me as a pupil, I did not lose heart. His paintings are in our churches and palaces and I and all folk may see them. They have taught me many things, beauty of color most of all. The powerful drawings of Michelangelo and the glowing colors of Titian—they are for all to see. Now, I, too, have my house looking out towards Murano, where fragile Venetian glass is blown, and I have my pupils. You shall come to me, Domenicos, and see my Marietta, and, like all others, you will take her as a fine young boy, since she dresses as a boy that she may help me in my workshop like my other pupils."

"You are kind, my Tintoretto, to such a lonely one as I—a Greek out of place in Venice. From your pictures I learn more than from those of the great Titian. The life in your portraits, the sureness and strength of your drawing, the surprises breaking through the patterns by others so placidly accepted, are an inspiration to me. Hours have I spent, oh, great Master, before your 'Presentation of the Little Virgin in the Temple,' that masterpiece which grew from your brushes when you were only twenty-eight. The depth, the light which illumines the picture and in so doing unifies it all, the glowing yellows and golden-browns contrasted with the crimsons and blues, are a constant joy, as well as the masterly way the little maiden holds the center of interest by her position with the attention of all others upon her. Would that I, oh, famous one, might be endowed with some of your vigor and power!"

El Greco held up his slender, white hands and sadly shook his head.

"Size of hands does not count in handling the brush, El Greco, but rather skill in the wielding of it, and the personality which goes from the painter to his canvas. You have it in you, boy. You will succeed, for already you have grown."

"There is coming to Rome a young student of Titian, El Greco, from the island of Crete, who, 'in my judgment is one of the very few who excel in painting; among other things, he has done a self portrait which has astonished all the artists here,'" wrote Don Giulio Clovio, called the "Michelangelo of Illuminators," to Cardinal Farnese, a patron of the arts in Rome.

"Domenicos shall study the drawings of the mighty Michelangelo. Perhaps he will feel more at home in Rome, a city more solemn, more stern, than sparkling Venice. And there is need of young artists there."

A few years later, El Greco, the strange young artist who had gone from Crete to study in Venice and in Rome, sailed for Spain.

"Ah, poor boy! so sensitive, so proud, so filled with visions and dreams," sighed some of his friends. "He will be more lonely in Spain—and yet, Italy was not the place for him. Will King Philip of Spain receive him well?"

El Greco knew at the very beginning of his stay in Spain that he belonged to Toledo, that city set high upon a granite rock, crowning it. Fascinated, his pale face alight, the Greek walked through the narrow streets, peered into the churches to see their solemn wall pictures, marveled at the treasures which the Moors had left behind. And just as the kind old book illuminator, Giulio Clovio, had said, Toledo needed a painter. Sculptors she had and glass painters, ivory workers and goldsmiths, but great painters of pictures had been lacking and would be welcomed, if they would only make live the history and the greatness of Spain.

El Greco became famous in Toledo. He was commissioned to decorate many churches, to paint the portraits of the well-known of that time. And just as he captured the likeness of the gentle old book illuminator, Clovio, in so sympathetic a manner that we seem to know him, so did he reveal the true likenesses of the noted ones of Spain. "He was in all things as singular as in his painting," was said of him. He introduced "such an extravagant style that to this day nothing has been seen equal to it."

"The lightnings will soon be flashing, my father. Shall we not turn around and go home?" reasoned Jorge Manuel, El Greco's son, as he stood by his father's side, watching him paint the city of Toledo perched high on a rock.

El Greco stepped back from his canvas and looked at the granite hill upon which Toledo stood, and at the threatening sky above. Even as he looked, forked lightnings flashed across that cloud-banked sky, lighting the roofs and towers, rising up towards the hilltops in sharp lines.

Then he shook his head, while his brush played swiftly over his canvas.

"Ah, no! Jorge Manuel. I have been waiting for just such a storm-sky, which has these colors—strange greens and cold blues, threatening colors growing darker as they do now. I'm even going to capture the stillness before the coming storm. See, even the olive leaves are motionless. If you are going to be an artist one day, Jorge Manuel, as you say now you want to be, you mustn't tremble before a storm. Behold! into this picture will go a part, at least, of the power and beauty of that stormy sky, the bluish-whites and strange greens, the lightning's flash, the stillness of the moment with the feeling of the crash about to come. A poem it shall be, Jorge Manuel, with these colors the verses—a poem to the strange, mysterious dream-city, Toledo, which has become our home."

PETER PAUL RUBENS

1577–1640

BEFORE THE STORY

ALTHOUGH Peter Paul Rubens was not born in Antwerp, his lawyer father had been an alderman there until, because of religious persecution by the Spaniards, he was forced to flee to Cologne. When Peter Paul was ten years old, and after his father's death, they went back there to live. There it was that he first studied to become a painter. So Antwerp, a very old and busy town of Belgium, is always connected with the painter, Rubens, who helped make it famous.

Some day you will enjoy visiting it with its magnificent Cathedral, its fine harbor, its beautiful paintings, many of which are by this very painter.

Supposing we view a little picture gallery of our own before we hear about this great artist who created them. With some of them I am quite sure you are already familiar.

He painted portraits of himself, studying his face in a mirror, and looking very determined and capable of doing great things. Many portraits he painted of great people whose characters he imprisoned upon his canvas: archbishops, kings, queens, decorating a gallery in Paris with pictures of the life of Marie de' Medici, Regent of France. Most of all we will enjoy his pictures of mothers and babies. Many of them are of the Holy Mother and Child, but just as real and human as his own wife and babies. No doubt Rubens often used his own wife and little son as models for his religious paintings, which perhaps helped to give them the wonderful quality they have of being alive. Besides, he always loved children, so he was able to paint them in his pictures with their plump little cheeks, chubby bodies, dimpled arms and legs, making us long to cuddle them in our arms.

He made the Holy Family like a happy earthly family, so natural and so joyous together. Those pictures are beautiful in composition as well as rich in color, each line, each gesture, each expression leading us to the baby and mother. And the colors! They glow and sing and sparkle, rich, deep red, vibrant tints of the flesh, greens and browns of the background which make the foreground colors all the more luminous.

Some of Rubens' Pictures:

HOLY FAMILY (*Madonna with a Parrot*)
Royal Museum, Antwerp
PORTRAITS OF HIS WIFE AND TWO CHILDREN
Louvre, Paris
HOLY FAMILY
Metropolitan Museum of Art, New York
VENUS AND ADONIS
Metropolitan Museum of Art, New York
SAINT CECELIA
Metropolitan Museum of Art, New York
THOMAS HOWARD, EARL OF ARUNDEL
Isabella Stewart Gardner Museum, Boston
QUEEN TOMYRIS
Museum of Fine Arts, Boston
RETURN FROM THE FLIGHT
Wadsworth Atheneum, Hartford

A PAGE WHO BECAME A PAINTER: PETER PAUL RUBENS OF ANTWERP

"He is a strange fellow, this Peter Paul who has but recently come to us," confided one velvet-jacketed page to another. " 'Tis said that his mother, knowing our Countess, wished him to be trained here. But what for? Quentin, Hans, Anton! dost see the training of a Squire, a Knight, a Courtier, a Lawyer, or a Diplomat in this new page of ours? Methinks he is born to be a dreamer rather than a doer. And so solemn-eyed he is that I am, forthwith, uneasy in his presence!"

"Tut, Jan," chided Quentin, as he busied himself in helping get the golden goblets ready for a banquet which the Countess Marguerite of Lalaing was holding on that night. "The new page might well be a diplomat, for he can argue a question from every side until the rest of us know not silver from steel! And look ye how the Countess favors him for his courtly manners, though in his duties as page he often falls far short."

"By the good Saint Martin, the patron of all brave knights!" added Anton, "are not good manners the duty of every page if he would become a true knight? When the accolade of knighthood is given, the newly made knight vows to be chivalrous and courteous to all ladies!"

"Even so," shrugged Jan, "I repeat he is a strange lad, different from the rest of us—for better or for worse, who knows? And how strange it sounds to be calling him 'Peter' and 'Paul' as if we were summoning the apostles!"

"How say'st thou, Master Jan?" asked the new page under discussion, walking into their midst quite unconcernedly, holding one of the basins for the washing of hands at the banquet. "Mayhap my names sound strange, for I bear not the name of my father nor his sire, but of the holy apostles Peter and Paul. I was born, my mother tells me, on the eve of their feast day."

"One fair lady will call thee 'Sir Peter' when thou art knighted, and another 'Sir Paul'!" laughed Anton. "Thou wilt become two knights in one! Dost not like it here as page in the castle of our fair lady, the Countess Marguerite? Thou art so solemn-eyed."

Peter Paul's face clouded and his dark, expressive eyes looked far away, while one slipper seemed to be tracing a strange pattern upon the floor. "The reading of Latin, the playing upon the lute and the singing, the learning to write the Latin letters with the brush—that I like. When the castle scribe lets me decorate the manuscript page with little pictures in rich colors and ofttimes in gold, and border patterns and big initial letters beginning the Latin texts—that I love! But the banquets, the rivalry in the castle—they please me not."

"But such merrymaking we have!" gasped Quentin. "Look ye, good Peter Paul, on this very night at the banquet, so I overheard the steward say, there is to be a mighty pie which at the word of our lady will be cut open and fiddlers will appear ready to give forth their sweet music for the guests. Does not that enliven thee? And upon this red and gold cloth of the banquet table are to be figures of falcons which beat their wings like those we carry upon our wrists when we go riding to the hunt. And all sorts of strange devices."

"Do we not have tilting enough at the joust or tournament to please thee, Peter Paul?" asked Anton. "With all the gay tents of the challengers, the bright banners waving, the armor gleaming, plumes dancing, and lances clashing, there is excitement always in the air. Hast worn thy suit of armor yet and tried thy foot in the stirrups, thy hand at the lance?"

Before Peter Paul could answer, Hans pounced upon him. "Mayhap it is the carving he likes not, for truly the peacock and partridge are stubborn and tricky to carve. But even a squire must do that and taste from the meat and the cup before serving. I know! thou dost already long for the day when thou shalt be knight, have pages to bring thee thy goblet, a squire to see to thy armor, and a fair lady for whom to contend in the tourney!"

"If thou dost dream of becoming churchman, doctor, lawyer, or courtier," offered Jan, looking earnestly at the downcast face of the new page who seemed not at all to relish their antics, their merrymaking, their banquets, "where canst thou get better training in manners than here in our Lady's castle, to add to the learning thou hast already acquired in the Jesuit School? Here thou wilt learn also to speak the French tongue, which will serve thee well as a diplomat!" finished Jan triumphantly.

Peter Paul at that threw back his head and smiled, and the smile seemed to play in his eyes as well as on his lips. "You are kind, fellow pages, and frank, so will I also be frank with you. The merrymaking and banqueting pleased me well at first, but I weary of it as the days go by. 'God-speed' I must say, bowing low, each time I enter the great hall to help wait upon the Countess and her guests, and forthwith bow my knees and hold the goblet for drinking or the bowl for hand washing or the platter piled high with pastries or meats. I must go hawking and hunting whenever my knight and my squire shall decide; sing, dance, wear armor and learn how to joust; even play the game of chess to entertain the ladies whenever they wish, to say naught of the many and sundry errands I must run. Nay, 'tis not what interests me most and I would beg my good mother to let me go home."

"Nay, do not go!" gasped Jan, aghast, while the others stood gazing, speechless. "Soon wilt thou be squire, one step nearer the goal of knighthood, and anon, Peter Paul, will come the day when thou wilt receive the accolade, or blow of knighthood, and mayhap serve king or queen. Then thou wilt be Sir Peter Paul!"

"Thou speakest well, friend Jan, and thy eloquent words I commend. Hark ye! I aim not to be knight, or courtier, or lawyer. Diplomat I might well have to be if I fulfil the dream in my heart. For I would be a painter of pictures, Jan. I would make pictures so real, so natural, that Nature might claim them as her own; so rich in color that they delight the eye. I will capture in my pictures king, queen, courtiers, as well as mothers and babies for the holy pictures of the church. One day you will see. And speaking of knighthood, who knows but what some king or some queen will say to me, 'Kneel, Peter Paul, I will give thee the accolade because of thy pictures which will live in the years to come. Rise, Sir Peter Paul Rubens—knighted for thy art!' Who knows?"

Just as a knight of chivalry was determined to win his spurs so Peter Paul Rubens made up his mind to become the sort of painter of pictures he desired to be. Eagerly he trained in the studios of artists in Antwerp, studied the works of great artists in Rome and in Venice, going through his apprenticeship, until he had a workshop of his own, and a busy one it was.

"Early to bed and early to rise, maketh one healthy and wealthy—it may be—but cross instead of wise!" yawned one of his young assistants who, in helping the Master, was learning to paint. "No workshop in Antwerp is astir so early, and no master has such an appetite for work as ours. Woe be unto the laggard in the Rubens' studio. One would think he was contending in a race!"

"Bridle thy tongue, Frans," chided another young assistant. "Where should we be without the most wonderful master in the world? We may labor all day and cover much canvas but the result is naught without the magic touch of the Master to give it life and beauty."

"Thou art right, Paul," conceded Frans, "and I meant no harm. Well do I know of our master's genius and proud I am of the honors he has already received—court painter to the Duke of Mantua, to the Archduke Albert and the Infanta Isabella of the Netherlands. No doubt he will receive even greater honors. But come! we must not spend the moments in gossip but must work at the master's designs for these many pictures which have been ordered, so that they may be ready for his magic touch. But look—here comes Master Rubens now!"

The sun was just rising as Rubens took up his brushes and palette, pausing to bid his pupils a cheery good morning and to caress his wife and small son, who peered cautiously in, and then hastened away that they might not disturb him at work.

"Come, Cornelis!" he called, as he made ready his scheme of colors and with sure, deft strokes attacked the great canvas which must be finished on that day. "Read to me now while I paint, that all senses may work together and no precious moments may be lost. Let us go on with that chapter in Cicero we were reading yesterday. Should my good helper and pupil, young Anton van Dyck, come, send him to me at once, for I have need of his work, and I would have him look over with me my treasures in art, an hour before the midday meal."

"A sane mind in a sane body," the old Greek ideal of life, was his also, and this he fulfilled. There were no minutes wasted, though it was not all work.

"Saddle the gray horse I rode yesterday," he commanded, when the day was waning. "I would chase away my weariness by a gallop through the countryside, and be back in plenty of time to receive the good Burgomaster. It has been a full day, and the lines and colors of beauty have flowed from my brush's tip. I can scarce wait for more work on the morrow."

"Think of it!" his pupils and assistants murmured some years after that, "our master is being sent by the Infanta Isabella as ambassador to the court of His Majesty, King Philip of Spain, who has long admired his work. Is that not the highest of honors? There he will meet the Spanish court painter, Diego Velazquez, who paints such marvelous likenesses of the court, so rumor has it. Our Master, Peter Paul Rubens, will more than hold his own, and no doubt will be engaged on many a day in painting the court ladies. Meanwhile we will serve him by trying to keep on the work here at home."

How they did laugh when the report reached them that one day a Spanish courtier, rather superior in manner, came upon the Flemish painter, whose fame he knew not, busy at his easel. "What! does an ambassador to his Catholic Majesty amuse himself with painting pictures?" he questioned. "No," answered Rubens, "the painter sometimes amuses himself with diplomacy."

"I would have given much to have heard him," chuckled Jan. "Peter Paul Rubens is a match for anyone! 'Tis said that when he was page in the castle of the Countess his manners in performing his duties endeared him to her, and his fellow pages foretold he would be a good diplomat. He will grace any court and will win for himself world renown. The coming spring will see him an envoy sent from Spain to the Court of England, where new honors await him. Hold up your heads, lads. Anton, do you hasten to the market place to let his honors be known. He is the greatest painter of all lands!"

"Hast heard?" one who had been a fellow page in the castle with the boy Peter Paul asked of another who had also been there. "Even though he left the training of the school of chivalry, he has been knighted and with greater honors than any of us ever received. His Majesty, King Charles the First of England, gave him the accolade of knighthood with a jeweled sword in return for his services as envoy between England and Spain, and because of his pictures. 'Rise, Sir Petrus Paulus Rubens!' he said to him, and forthwith further honored him by giving him a ring from his royal finger and a hatband set in diamonds! Truly, he has far surpassed us."

"Just as surely has he made his boyhood dreams come true," added another. "Blessed and happy is that one who holds steadfastly to his ideals. He has served not only his city of Antwerp and the Netherlands, but Italy, Spain, England, even the whole world by the beauty of the pictures which no one but he could paint. Health of body and mind gave him the balance which makes the diplomat; understanding eyes and mind and heart, knowledge of the secrets and beauties of Nature and the willingness to take infinite pains, made him a Knight in Art."

FRANS HALS

c. 1580–1666

BEFORE THE STORY

Holland is such a quaint, picturesque little country, that we don't at all wonder the Dutch folk love it—every inch of the low-lying, yellow-green fields, the canals gay with boats laden with many a fine cargo and borne from the sea by their white and colored sails; the dikes or high walls of stone and earth which keep back the sea from the land which, strangely enough it seems to us, is lower than the besieging waters.

A network of canals crosses the fields, carrying water to them, and making the little country look almost like a great checkerboard; canals serve the purpose of streets and are crossed by little bridges. Canals frozen over in the winter time are crowded with happy people skating to market, to school, to church! No hills relieve the flatness of the country, but windmills make interesting silhouettes with their outstretched arms against the cloud-swept sky and are busy pumping water from the land and grinding corn. Gay little red and yellow brick gabled houses reflect the bright sunlight almost like mirrors, so clean, so polished they are, just as much on the outside as on the inside, and framed in colorful gardens. Tulip and narcissus beds gayly bloom amidst the green, and beautiful shade trees form long, straight rows on one side of the canal, bowing to the shining houses on the other! The clatter of wooden shoes on the cobbles, the flash of light on red and blue skirts and white-winged caps—all this is picturesque Holland!

Do you wonder that the Dutch boys and girls are happy? Do you wonder that all the Dutch folk love the land which they worked so hard to save from the sea, watching the dikes very carefully lest there should be a little leak growing into a big and bigger one and letting the ocean through into their fields and homes? And do you wonder that the Dutch artists loved to make very truthful and beautiful pictures of the everyday scenes and everyday people around them? Whatever and whomever we have to work for and care for we cherish; the Dutch people have always cherished their country they saved from the sea and their independence they saved from the Spanish who once ruled over them. Through their happy and truthful pictures of their home life and their portraits, they have showed the charm of Holland to the world.

An artist of Holland, next to Rembrandt in skill and in truth, is the jolly Frans Hals. He was born some time between 1580 and 1584 and as a boy lived in Antwerp but later moved to Haarlem with his parents. There, his father was a municipal magistrate, and Frans, himself, was made a member of the Civic Guard and of the Guild of Rhetoric. Also, he was one of the Directors of the Guild of Saint Lucas, interested in all the arts and crafts in Haarlem. This I am telling you so that you will see that he was a respected citizen of Haarlem, and not a fellow who spent all of his time in the tavern! It is true that he did like to go there to watch the expressions upon the faces of the jolly fellows he met, and no doubt he drank and laughed and joked and chatted with them, joining with them in singing songs and telling stories, watching their faces with the idea of making their likenesses live upon his canvases.

You will see them in his pictures. But never did he let his good times with his rollicking comrades interfere with his splendid pictures.

So quickly he painted that you can see the brush strokes, and such lifelike figures his brushes produced in such very real-looking clothes, appearing to the eyes the way they would feel to the fingers—delicate lace, heavy broadcloth, velvet or muslin. He could make up his mind at a glance just what he wanted to portray, and imprison it upon his canvas, the vivid expression of a moment or two.

Although Frans Hals did not have the imagination and deep thought of Rembrandt, the grace of Sir Anthony van Dyck, or the dignity of Velazquez, yet jolly Frans Hals was a very skilful and wonderful portrait painter, making live upon his canvases the practical, loyal, and brave Dutch folk, and their everyday life.

Some of Frans Hals' Works:

THE MERRY DRINKER
Ryks Museum, Amsterdam

PORTRAIT OF A MAN
Metropolitan Museum of Art, New York

THE MERRY COMPANY
Metropolitan Museum of Art, New York

YONKER RAMP AND HIS SWEETHEART
Metropolitan Museum of Art, New York

AN OLD WOMAN SEATED
National Gallery of Art, Washington

PORTRAIT OF AN OFFICER
National Gallery of Art, Washington

Balthasar Coymans
National Gallery of Art, Washington
Boy Playing a Flute
Collection of Edward Drummond Libbey, Toledo, Ohio
Portrait of Heer Bodolphe
Collection of John Pierpont Morgan, New York

A JOLLY DUTCHMAN WHO PAINTED PICTURES: FRANS HALS

Elizabeth Van der Meer was busy scrubbing the outside of her red-brick house in Haarlem. Even the fourteen-year-old daughter of the Burgomaster of Haarlem, Nicolaes Van der Meer, had her daily tasks to perform, and the outside of the house must be just as bright as the inside, so Elizabeth's mother and all other Dutch housewives insisted. Jacob and Hendrik were scrubbing, too, freeing their wooden shoes from every speck of dirt, and standing them in a row to dry in the warm sunlight which flooded their courtyard. Vrouw Van der Meer's maid was scrubbing the brick pavement outside of the house! Many a day had she scrubbed just as painstakingly though the rain fell, and Hendrik was persuaded to hold an umbrella over her head!

"Our life is a ship,
The world is the sea
The Bible our Compass,
But Heaven is our haven," *

sang the maidservant as she vigorously scrubbed.

* *From the flyleaf of an old Dutch Bible.*

"Tomorrow is my birthday and I am going visiting with the good father!" sang Elizabeth as she scrubbed and polished until every brick that she could reach, shone. "And I, too," echoed Jacob eagerly, watching the sun quickly dry his shoes. Hendrik did not even hear; his thoughts were with the treasure-laden, red-sailed ships he had seen that morning coming in from the far seas. He was going to be a sailor, and bring back from the far east some of the shining silks and patterned rugs such as he had seen when he went with his father to visit the old captain who had fought against the Spanish foe upon the sea, and he had fearlessly helped to save. The rug he had sold Father and which now covered the table in the parlor beneath the high window was rich in color and pleasing in pattern, and Hendrik never tired feeling of it and looking at it.

All three, leaving their wooden shoes outside, went indoors. There, too, everything was very bright and shining and in perfect order. No one ever tossed a cap or scarf on chair or table; everything was in place. The high-backed chairs stood up very primly almost like mirrors in the way their shining surfaces reflected the light; even as the copper and bronze kettles and pots and long-handled warming pan hanging above the deep fireplace. The floor had little diamond-shaped patterns all over it, and in the parlor it was sanded and formed into patterns. Grandmother was sitting at one corner of the fireplace where the light from the white-curtained window shone directly upon her as she wrinkled up her forehead and leaned over to smooth her thread, peering over her glasses as she always did. Every once in a while she gently rocked the hooded cradle, then back again she turned to the skilful spinning of which she was so proud. Grandfather puffed on his long-stemmed pipe, blinked, snoozed, then stretched, and went out to sit in the sunshine-flooded courtyard.

Elizabeth drew more closely together the long curtains which concealed the bed built right into the wall, then hurried to find Vrouw Van der Meer. Jacob went outside again and was soon clattering away in his spotless wooden shoes. Hendrik went softly into the parlor, taking great care not to disturb the sand patterns upon the floor. The light brought out the deep blue, the rich red of the rug draped upon the table. It shone upon the brass pitcher and bowl, upon the big map hanging upon one wall. "Persia," gloated Hendrik, "and India, that's where I am going!"

Elizabeth wondered where they were going the next day, though she did not ask. It was enough that it was her birthday and that she was walking along the canal in her new, full, red skirt, her jacket trimmed with fur, and her bonnet-like cap which reached down at the sides to meet her broad white collar. Jacob, dressed just like his father though only one-fourth as large, also silently walked along. Hendrik had preferred to stay at home.

"Well, my young ones," boomed Heer Van der Meer's big voice, "we are nearly there. Once thou dost step into yonder gabled house, thou wilt have two fathers!"

Two fathers! Puzzled, Elizabeth glanced at Jacob, who, hands in the pockets of his wide trousers, was plodding sturdily along, trying to take as big steps as his tall father, the honored Burgomaster of Haarlem. He merely shrugged. 'Twas not like his good father to make such a joking remark, or so it sounded, right where everyone was passing them along the main canal, and bowing so politely to their good burgomaster. It was a very strange remark, and Elizabeth glanced again at the tall, bulky person by her side, his face seeming to flower from the stiff, frilled ruff. A long, heavy cape hung well back over his shoulders, his broad-brimmed black hat was constantly removed with great dignity as he graciously returned the greetings of the good folk of Haarlem. No, her father was not joking; of that she was certain.

"Tie the splendid Orange, Orange still above!" sang a booming voice. "Ja, ja! In memory of our Duke William of Orange, who won for us our freedom from the Spanish grandees—now, my good friends, join me in raising the glasses high!" A rollicking song, then hearty cheers, followed by talking and laughter. To their utter amazement, Elizabeth and Jacob saw their dignified father hesitate, take a few steps towards the open door of the Haarlem town house or tavern, hesitate, frown, then walk resolutely away, and so quickly that they had to hurry to keep up with him.

That strange remark—that hesitating before the tavern door—Elizabeth's mind was in a whirl! No, it could not be, not her good and dignified father who had often bemoaned the wasted hours spent by the happy-go-lucky, roistering fellows who frequented that very tavern.

"Here we are, my children, before the house of Frans Hals, of Haarlem. Ach! here is Juvrouw Sara to let us into the master's room."

Elizabeth and Jacob smiled and nodded shyly to the girl, no older than they, who ushered them into the room flooded with clear light from a high, north window, and filled with many curious things.

"Hendrik will be sorry he did not come," Elizabeth whispered to Jacob as she caught sight of a beautiful Persian rug. "This is even more lovely than the one Mynheer the shipmaster brought our good father."

Then Elizabeth gasped and looked at her brother, who stood with mouth wide open, blinking at her! There was their father, Mynheer Nicolaes Van der Meer, Burgomaster of Haarlem, standing with one hand resting upon the back of an upholstered chair, the other carefully holding his gloves, his face framed by the stiff, pleated ruff, peering intently at them. On the other hand, there he was, a little farther away in a more shadowy corner of the room, standing in just the same position, even to the way the gauntlet gloves were held, and gazing straight at them with just the same intent expression that they knew so well.

Jacob rubbed his eyes and, walking up to the nearer figure, touched the hand resting upon the back of the chair. It was real flesh and blood, and he distinctly saw a twinkle in his father's eyes, though there was no movement of the body! Elizabeth walked over close to the other figure in the corner. Closer to it she went and put out her hand just as her eyes informed her. "Ho!" she chuckled. "You have the real father and I his double upon canvas! Thou didst indeed play a rare joke upon us, my father!"

" 'Tis true, there are two fathers here," laughed Jacob, "but I choose the real one!"

"Mynheer Frans Hals is a great painter," answered their father. "So swift he is, making this likeness with only a few sittings, so sure and so truthful. 'Tis done at the request of the burghers of Haarlem," he added proudly.

"Such a fine birthday surprise it is," declared Elizabeth. "But where is Mynheer Hals, whose work it is?"

"Ach! that is the trouble," sighed her father, seating himself in the chair. "One never can tell when he will forget himself at the tavern. No real harm does he do, no drinking which would take away his skill as a painter of portraits, but the love of a good story, a rollicking song, a hearty laugh, a toast to his country and friends. Hail fellow, well met! But, methinks I shall give that jolly fellow a piece of my mind for keeping me waiting on this day which he set aside for the finishing of my portrait. Come, sit ye down in patience for a time. If he comes not soon, his son or his daughter shall go to the tavern and remind him that he has work to do. But little cares the jolly master painter, Mynheer Frans Hals, whom he keeps waiting—whether it be a fishwife of Haarlem or his burgomaster!"

There was plenty in the master's studio for their eyes to feast upon. There was a laughing mandolin player holding up a glass in one hand, his jolly smile showing him to be a merry fellow on right good terms with the world; the laughing cavalier, his smile ready to burst into a hearty laugh at any moment; a proud, white-capped nurse holding up in her arms a lace-bonneted baby, its chubby face rippling into happy laughter over its broad lace collar and stiff, flowered gown; a group of officers seated at a table, hands and faces full of varied expressions, so natural that they seemed to be actually seated there!

Such marvelous portrait studies, catching the expressions of the moment, sometimes appearing as if they were about to change right before their eyes. Such truth in putting upon his canvases what his eyes saw, just so far as he could. Such swift strokes, in a flash seeing just what he wanted to make last upon his canvas, and imprisoning it there. And such skill in making lace seem to be formed of delicate threads, flesh soft to the touch, a harmony of grays and blacks. Above all, such life to all the figures.

So absorbed they were that at first they were quite unaware that a tall, dignified, graceful young man had entered the room. "The painter—Frans Hals?" he inquired.

His very appearance, the cobweb lace of his collar, the rich velvet of his cape, the silver buckles on his slippers, the plume on his soft, broad hat, his cavalier manner, his way of speaking, all told the same story; he must be some very wealthy stranger!

"I have heard of the great painter, Frans Hals of Haarlem," he said with a courtly bow, "and of his masterly portraits. I am from another country and would take back to my people this master's skill. Just two hours are at my disposal in which to sit for my portrait. Will you kindly summon the painter at once?"

Elizabeth and Jacob looked at each other in dismay. Mynheer the Burgomaster looked at the stranger in amazement. He quite forgot his own impatience at the artist's delay in keeping his appointment with him. He thought only of the fame of his countryman, which was at stake unless they could get him at once to paint the portrait of this wealthy and distinguished young man. Yet, how were they to manage it? It would never do to let him know that Mynheer Frans Hals was having a jolly time in the tavern! He would never understand that he went to study the merry fellows he met there, the ever-changing expressions which flitted across their faces, that he might picture them upon his canvases. With a suave excuse to account for the painter's absence, introducing himself with much dignity as the Burgomaster of Haarlem, he promised that the stranger's portrait should be painted forthwith! In a very gracious yet dignified manner, he begged to be excused for the moment.

The eyes of Elizabeth and Jacob followed him in admiration. Their good father was every bit as distinguished as the important looking stranger! But was he going to the tavern to fetch Mynheer Frans Hals?

The burgomaster and the painter's daughter Sara were in a whispered consultation. She was already stepping into her wooden shoes, when they heard a hearty voice say, "Ach! the reproaches of the good burgomaster will be upon my head for my lateness," and the painter himself hurried in. "What is all this—?" he began, only to be hushed by a peremptory shake of the head by the burgomaster himself. With many gestures and mysterious whispering, they hurried him into his workroom, and soon he was rapidly painting his unknown guest, who watched with keen interest each stroke of the brush.

Mynheer Frans Hals was at his best. His brush fairly flew over the canvas, bold, sure, vigorous strokes making the strange and aristocratic young man live upon his canvas, until as Jacob whispered, there were two guests in the room! No stroke that was not needed, and each full of meaning; each color taking its place in happy relationship to its neighbor, the rich black velvet cape not dull but catching the lights, the plume of the hat making the fingers itch to touch its white softness. And the eyes of the stranger, so farseeing, as if they saw all at a glance.

"The best portrait thou hast painted, my good friend, Frans Hals," commented the burgomaster impressively, as the painter was giving the portrait the last, few, sure touches.

"Within the two hours," commented the stranger. "It is a fine likeness, Sir Painter. Surely, painting is an easier thing than I thought. Let us change places, for my time is not yet up, and see what I can do!"

What a strange request! But Frans Hals, with his usual jolly laugh, produced a fresh canvas, and gave him paint and clean brushes, and his own palette. He was always fond of a joke.

"Thou art no stranger in handling brushes," he observed as his guest set to work. The minutes flew, and the portrait of the Dutch painter, Frans Hals, grew and lived on the canvas. Those in the room watched, breathless. Who could their guest be?

"There," smiled the stranger, "it is finished, and in less time than yours, though to my mind not so lifelike. How dost thou like thy portrait, Frans Hals?"

The Dutch painter looked long at the swiftly painted portrait, long at the smiling man who created it. Then he sprang to his feet and went forward with outstretched hand. "The man who can do that, must be either Van Dyck or the devil!" he exclaimed.

The stranger laughed. "It pleases me most to be Van Dyck!" he retorted.

"The great Sir Anthony Van Dyck!" murmured Mynheer Frans Hals, bowing before him. "The renowned painter who will make live forever all his fellow countrymen!"

"What a wonderful birthday I have had," exulted Elizabeth as they walked homeward along the canal, quite some hours later, after the painter had also finished the burgomaster's portrait. "Our jolly painter and the court painter of England were surely well matched. How sorry Hendrik will be that he stayed at home!"

ANTHONY VAN DYCK

1599–1641

BEFORE THE STORY

WHENEVER we look at Van Dyck's picture of three of the children of King Charles the First, of England, which is included among the illustrations in this book, we think how contented and happy they seem to be. Not a bit like the princes and princesses of Spain who look so stiff and forlorn and unhappy. Though they are dressed very strangely it seems to us, in silk and satin frocks, lace collars and caps, yet they seem to be real boys and girls, not puppets of the court as the Royal Children of Spain look to be. Van Dyck made the people of the royal court live, and the painting of their portraits made him famous.

Though Van Dyck spent some years of his life in England, he was Flemish by birth, being born in Antwerp in 1599, the son of a wealthy silk merchant. Showing very early his gift for painting, he received the best training from the age of ten, and studied with Rubens.

After a while, Anthony grew restless in Rubens' studio and wanted to start out for himself and see the wonders of other cities. So, at the advice of Rubens, he went on a trip to Italy, where he enjoyed and studied the pictures of the great Italian painters, especially those of the Venetian artists, Titian's most of all. Rubens, his teacher, had given him letters of introduction, and in Genoa, especially, he was asked to paint portraits of nobles, fine ladies, warriors, church dignitaries. Four years he stayed in Italy and then went back to his own city of Antwerp, to paint pictures for his own land, where burghers and their wives wanted him to paint their portraits. Everyone liked them very much; many thought them better than Rubens' because he gave to them such charm and dignity, and put so much expression and character into their faces.

Van Dyck established and superintended a school of painting in Antwerp until he was called by King Charles the First to come to England as his court painter. He died at the early age of forty-two in London.

This story I am about to tell you now has to do in fact and fancy with the great English court painter, Van Dyck, who lived over two hundred years ago, and with the royal people whom he made live for us on canvas. Although some of the people in it may not have spoken and acted in just this way, it is all true to the history and spirit of the times.

Some Pictures by Sir Anthony Van Dyck:

CHARLES THE FIRST AND HENRIETTA MARIA
Pitti Gallery, Florence
CHARLES THE FIRST, KING OF ENGLAND
Louvre, Paris
WILLIAM II, PRINCE OF ORANGE AND HIS BRIDE, PRINCESS MARY
Ryks Museum, Amsterdam
JAMES STUART, DUKE OF LENNOX
Metropolitan Museum of Art, New York
THE MARCHESA GRIMALDI
National Gallery of Art, Washington
PORTRAIT OF A LADY
Metropolitan Museum of Art, New York

Queen Henrietta Maria
Fine Arts Gallery, San Diego, California
The Earl of Arundel and His Grandson
Metropolitan Museum of Art, New York

ANTHONY VAN DYCK, COURT PAINTER TO KING CHARLES THE FIRST OF ENGLAND

It was a time of great festivity in London, in the month of May, in the year 1660, and the English people were very glad to have festivities and merrymaking, and a cause for rejoicing, for they were tired of all the quarrelings and unrest and killings of the last twenty years. "Down with the Commonwealth!" the English people had been crying for some time. "Let us bring back Prince Charles! Better times there were in his reign!" Not at all to their liking had been the stern rule of Oliver Cromwell, and they were weary of being governed by an army which was always at war with Parliament. "Punishment has come upon us in these troubled times for the shedding of royal blood!" they decided, thinking with regret of the beheading of their King, Charles the First. "We have had no Commonwealth, but a Kingdom with Oliver Cromwell our ruler as much as King Charles ever was! Let us bring back the son of King Charles that we may have joyful days once more! Down with the Commonwealth! God save the King!"

Prince Charles, who had escaped to France, and who had already been crowned King by the loyal Scots, was recalled to England, and from him came promises of pardon to those who had turned against his father, and the promise of the right of all to worship as they willed. On the 29th of May, in 1660, Charles the Second returned from exile.

Such a shouting and cheering as there was! The streets were strewn with flowers, tapestries were hung from the fronts of the houses, gay banners and streamers waved from the windows. There were fountains of wine to the great delight of many, and there was a long procession ablaze with gold and silver, rich velvets and many colored banners. Trumpets sounded and all the people at their sound gathered in the streets, ladies leaned far out of their windows or even stood upon the roofs to see the return of their Prince, and watch the great crowds of people passing through the city for seven hours' time. One of those who saw the long procession wrote in his diary, "so glorious was the show with gold and silver, that we were not able to look at it, our eyes at last being so overcome."

In April 1661, came the great celebration, the Coronation Day of Charles the Second in Westminster Abbey. All London gathered to see the royal procession pass. There were lords, knights, heralds, dukes, stewards, constables, footmen, chamberlains, soldiers of the guard and many other officers and gentlemen, over twenty thousand on horse and on foot, all rich in embroidery, cloth of silver and of gold, velvet and jewels. Charles the Second was placed on a throne above the altar and the Bishop of London asked the people if they would give their loyalty to their King. "God save King Charles the Second, who now has returned to his people!" shouted the vast throng, again and again, and the King vowed to "maintain the Religion, Magna Charta, and Laws of the Land," after which he was anointed and crowned.

"Never before have I listened to such rare organ music," murmured a tall girl as she passed out of the church with her mother. "Such wonderful anthems and rich melodies! And the lutes, the viols, and the trumpets! It must be wonderful to be a king, and be honored and loved by all the people. Mother, this makes me want to hear again the story of my father and his life at the court of our new King's father. Tell me again tonight just as you used to tell me when I was just a little girl. Please, do, Mother!"

So that night, while the city was alive with the rejoicing of its many people at the return of their exiled prince, now crowned Charles the Second, and the sky was alight from time to time with the glare of huge bonfires and blazing torches, and the air filled with the ringing of bells and the blasts of trumpets, a mother and her daughter sat by the open window of their home in Blackfriars. There was no light inside, but the flames of the bonfires brightened the room, and showed the stout, oak, "X" shaped, upholstered chairs, and those with high seats and open backs ending in carved acorns or elaborate scrolls, with a carved, hooped stretcher between the front legs, a style borrowed from Flanders, from which country Sir Anthony Van Dyck had come. The mother was seated on one of these heavily carved chairs, her daughter on a low footstool at her knee.

"Now begin, Mother, just as you used to when I was only about so high, only tell me more; so 'Once upon a time'!"

The mother smiled and began obediently, "Well, then, Justiniana, 'once upon a time,' your father was court painter to King Charles the First of our land of England, and everyone held in high esteem Sir Anthony Van Dyck. You are like your father, Justiniana, in your desire for choice clothes, and your love of music, as well as in your features. He was born in Antwerp and he has often told me how he used to sit by his mother's side and watch her at her embroidery, for skill in which she was well known.

She it was who gave him his first lessons in drawing. 'My first delight in color came from my father, who was a glass painter before he became a silk merchant, so you see I was blessed in both my parents,' your father would often say.

"Later came his training in the studio of his master, the great Flemish painter, Peter Paul Rubens, who soon saw your father's gifts. But such pranks as the apprentice boys used to play! One day, while the master, Rubens, was out riding on one of his famous horses—which he knew how to ride so well and to paint so well that they looked as if they were filled with life—his pupils stole into his private studio and took a peep at one of the paintings on which he had been working. One of the boys was pushed against the still wet canvas and rubbed against the wet paint on the arm and chin of a Holy Mother. Imagine the consternation and dismay of the guilty boys! 'Young Anthony Van Dyck can repaint it,' they cried, 'for he can paint better than any of us!' So your father took his brushes, his hand trembling so that he could scarcely hold them, and quickly repainted the damaged picture. He then stole away for the night, dreading the next day and the master's wrath. In the morning Rubens walked in at his accustomed hour and hastened to look at the picture upon which he was working. 'That arm and chin,' said he, 'are by no means the poorest part of yesterday's work.' Later when he did discover that the picture had been tampered with, he readily overlooked the fault, so well was the painting done, and more and more did he give your father drawings to make for his pictures and parts of the painting to do."

"Now tell me about the court of King Charles when Father went there," begged Justiniana, anxious to hear that part of the story.

"There it was that your father and I met," answered Lady Van Dyck, smiling rather wistfully, filled with the longing to make live over again those happy days. "You know that I was Mary Ruthven then, and my father was the Earl of Gore, so I was one of the ladies of the Court and had the honor of being governess to the Royal Children. One morning I was helping the Prince of Wales, now our newly crowned King, with his Latin. The tapestries, always a-shimmer with their gold and silver threads, were drawn aside, and the King himself, the Queen, your father and the Earl of Arundel, who had always been a good friend to the court painter, walked into the room of the palace, the Queen's apartment, where the Royal Children were always taught their lessons. It was not so gloomy as the room where the Royal Children of Spain sat for their pictures, although the ceiling was just as high, the floor of black and white marble, the walls paneled in oak in patterns of fruit and flowers. The ceiling was richly modeled in plaster, and upon the walls were more cheerful pictures by the court painter. French hangings were bright with gold and silver threads, and plenty of light entered the room from the long windows."

"How did the King look, Mother?" interrupted Justiniana, who was only eight when the King's life was taken.

"He was tall and slight, with auburn hair, and very fond of dress, as much so as your father. On that day his doublet of dove-gray was embroidered with pearls and gold, and his beautiful lace collar was fastened by two golden tassels."

"And the Queen?" suggested Justiniana eagerly, who always wanted to make for herself a complete picture.

"Beautiful Queen Henrietta Maria was robed as always in a bright, shimmering satin, on this day of white with knots of blue, and a very pretty picture she made as she crossed the room and stood against the rose velvet curtains at the long windows. She, too, wore a deep lace collar, and it was fastened with bands of pearls. At once she knelt down and lifted little James, then only two years old, and took him upon her knee, while the small Princess Mary stood by her side. Charles, the Prince of Wales, was only five years old and still wore a frock and deep-pointed lace collar and cap. 'You are to have your pictures painted today, sweethearts,' announced King Charles, 'by Sir Anthony Van Dyck, whom you all know and hold as your friend.' Your father spent much of his time with the royal family, painting over and over again the King and Queen, and the Royal Children, with whom he was a great favorite.

"Meanwhile, I felt the eyes of Sir Anthony Van Dyck upon me, and after the King had formally presented the great painter to me, he added, and his eyes twinkled, 'Mary Ruthven, I trust that if these children prove restless you will do your best to keep them quiet, and that you will help my court painter to group them.' Your father bowed low before me; he was always very gracious and gallant in manner. Then with his assistant he began to get ready his brushes and his palette.

"The King, the Queen, and the good earl smilingly left the room, delighted at the way their little plan was working, for they had long been desirous of bringing Sir Anthony and me together. Then we grouped the children against a dark silken curtain, so dainty in their gay silk dresses. First stood the Prince of Wales with his hand on the head of his favorite dog, then the Princess Mary—bless her sweet ways!—who afterwards became the wife of William, Prince of Orange, and to the right, little James, the baby, with his chubby face peering out of his little lace cap. Children always liked your father for he was very gentle with them, and it was not his custom to work long at a time on each picture, but rather did he prefer making several different appointments on the same day.

"It seemed to me that day that never had I seen anyone work so fast; it was no time before he had sketched the figures with black and white chalk, always keeping the expressions of the children pleasing by his little stories of himself when he was a boy. He worked just an hour and then gave the picture to his assistant who was with him, bidding him have the childrens' costumes sent him so that he might work on the drapery from those. The Princess and Princes were loth to have him go. 'You promised you would tell us why you always wear that golden chain around your neck,' insisted Prince Charles; 'it shines and sparkles in the sunlight.'

" 'That was given me by your father, His Highness the King,' answered Sir Anthony, 'and your father's portrait set in diamonds is at the end.'

" 'Did he give it to you on your birthday?' questioned Princess Mary, curiously. 'My dear father gave me a real horse on mine. What does it mean, Lady Mary?'

"There was nothing for me to do but to tell my royal charges that King Charles had given the golden chain and his portrait set in diamonds to his court painter when he knighted him as a token of his affection and esteem. 'That is why you call him *Sir* Anthony,' I added, feeling all the while that he was watching me, and knowing that I admired him even then. As the knights of old received the accolade of knighthood for their brave and loyal deeds, so did your father for serving his king so well in providing that he and his court should be long remembered."

"Did you marry Father at once, Mother?" asked Justiniana excitedly, for she had never before heard this part of the story.

"Not for several years," answered her mother, adding slowly, with the smile gone from her face, "and it was only a few years that I had him with me."

"But, Mother, you have not told me how Prince Charles escaped from England," interposed Justiniana quickly, knowing how the memory of her father's sudden death saddened her mother. "Each time I look at the portraits of him painted by my father, I think of the dangers the young Prince, now our King, met."

After a few moments Lady Van Dyck continued, "Our present King had many wonderful adventures when he was the Prince of Wales; he was telling some of them yesterday at the festivities after his arrival.

"Many hair-breadth escapes and exciting adventures Prince Charles had, and to the honor of the English people be it said that although the sum of a thousand pounds was offered for his capture, not one of the common folk or the nobles betrayed him, but each aided him in every way. Oliver Cromwell's agents tried their best to find him, but he escaped them all. He had made a brave fight for his throne aided by the loyal Scots, who crowned him King, but after long and terrible fighting at the battle of Worcester, he was overcome by Cromwell's well-trained 'Ironsides' and forced to flee for his life.

"So Prince Charles cut off his long hair, darkened his face and his hands and dressed like a peasant so that he bore little resemblance to a Prince. After long and hard journeys across the fields and hedges and ditches, under cover of darkness, they reached the home of a loyal subject whom Prince Charles felt he could trust. There he found one of his own officers in hiding and they consulted together as to what it was best to do. 'Let us not go deeply into the woods nearby, for I am sure Cromwell's soldiers will think of that and leave no hiding place unsearched,' the officer said. 'Rather let us climb into the leafy branches of that great oak tree yonder, on the very edge of the wood; there we will be concealed and we can see what is going on around us.' Prince Charles readily agreed and they hastily procured some bread and cheese from their host and climbed into the great oak tree where they were completely hidden from view but could look down through the leaves and see all that was taking place.

" 'Faith, and I rather enjoyed it,' declared His Highness yesterday. He was only twenty-one at the time and his spirits were high and boyish. 'We amused ourselves with peering down at them, and little did the searching parties know what "royal fruit" they might have found in that tree!' he added, laughing heartily as did we all, though we trembled at the thought of his danger. 'And we ate our bread and cheese right over their heads—they no doubt thinking there were squirrels in the tree!' went on the King. Today, Justiniana, did you not notice the oak leaves the people wore on their caps? They are to remind them of the royal oak which saved King Charles from his enemies.

"Another time Prince Charles put away his peasant's costume and dressed as a servant. The sister of a good royalist pretended that she was going to visit her sister near Bristol. 'Well,' commanded the colonel as they were ready to start, 'give your mistress your hand and help her to mount.' 'I showed my awkwardness in great style then,' declared the King, 'for I gave her the wrong hand, and the colonel's mother said to her son, "A fine horseman my daughter has!" ' It was customary for the groom to ride before the mistress, and scarcely two hours had they proceeded when the horse lost a shoe, and they were forced to stop at a smithy's. As the smith put on the shoe, the Prince said to him, 'Has aught happened lately of interest?'

'Naught save the defeat of the rascal Scots!' To that the Prince made answer: 'Tell me, have any of the English been taken?' 'Some,' answered the smith, as he worked away on the shoe, 'but the worst one of all, that rogue, Charles Stuart, has not yet been caught!' These, and many other adventures had the fleeing Prince until at last he escaped to a foreign land. His ready wit often saved him.

"If only your father might be here tonight to rejoice with us at the return to his own land and people of our King, whose portrait as Prince he painted! King Charles, long live His Majesty, will not have so famous a court painter, one who knew so well how to paint royal people, and to bring out the charm, the grace and the dignity of those whom he pictured. Dearest to me, however, are his pictures of the Royal Children. He understood and liked them so well. His Highness was speaking of it only yesterday as he stood before one of those pictures in the palace. 'Would that Sir Anthony were here to beautify my court and make it live for the years to come!' he cried."

"If only Father might be here tonight at the celebration of the crowning of King Charles, that little prince whom he used to paint so often!" echoed Justiniana Van Dyck, as she put her arm around her mother and together they stood by the window and watched the light from the brilliant bonfires.

DIEGO VELAZQUEZ

1599–1660

BEFORE THE STORY

SPAIN! Forever connected in the minds and hearts of American boys and girls with King Ferdinand and Queen Isabella, who were finally persuaded to listen to the dreams and the plans of Christopher Columbus.

Spain! calling forth pictures of the Moors and their stronghold, the Alhambra Palace, that palace so plain on the outside but so very, very beautiful within, ablaze with color in intertwining leaves and vines, deep purple, shadowy yellow and bright gold. Corridors, towers, rooms and courts surrounded by fragrant fruit trees; fountains sparkling in the golden sunshine and silvered in the moonlight! Many stories are connected with almost every court and garden, hall and tower. There was the Enchanted Soldier who appeared on St. John's Eve, so it was said; the Princesses Three who were imprisoned in a tall tower, two of them escaping with their knights, while the third lost the courage to go for fear of her father's wrath. She stayed within her tower and some say that you can still hear the soft music of her silver lute, when the delicate patterns of the arches are reflected like warm moonbeam laces.

Spain! the land of bright colors and sunshine, fragrant gardens filled with gay flowers and also with high adventure; of dancing to the tinkling music of the tambourines and guitars.

Spain! with its palaces and courts, its kings and queens, among them King Philip the Fourth, his Queen, and his Royal Children. They were fortunate in having at the court Velazquez, a painter who caught them in all their dignity and formality. Because of his portraits of them, those royal people are best remembered today.

Velazquez, son of a noble family of Spain, began his life in Seville, in the very same year that Anthony Van Dyck was born, and was destined to serve King Philip IV of Spain as court painter, in the same years that Van Dyck was serving King Charles the First of England, though Velazquez lived twenty years longer than Van Dyck.

As a boy, Velazquez made pictures whenever and wherever he could and when he was twenty-three years old, upon the advice of his teacher, he went to Madrid, where he could study the pictures which were being collected for its art gallery, the Prado, one of the best in Europe. Madrid, a military outpost in the time of the Moors, was growing rich from the wealth which went to Spain from the gold mines of Spain's newly conquered possessions.

When we look at the portraits by Velazquez we do not wonder that King Philip, as soon as he saw one of them, was eager to have him paint his likeness, or that he made up his mind that Velazquez should be his court painter. From that time on, Velazquez spent his life in the service of his King. The King sent him to Italy to purchase pictures and statues for his Art Gallery in Madrid, and relied on him to superintend the court festivities. When the Spanish Princess, Maria Theresa, married King Louis the Fourteenth of France, thus strengthening the peace which had been declared between Spain and France, it was Velazquez who planned all the ceremonies, the journey to the island in a little river separating France and Spain, the pomp and display. Just think! the Princess traveled with a cavalcade eighteen miles long! No wonder Velazquez became very tired, and caught a severe cold. Later he became ill with a fever and died. When we think of all that Velazquez did for his King, we are not surprised at the latter's grief over his loss when he died in 1660.

Some of Velazquez' Paintings:

THE PRINCESS MARIA THERESA
Prado, Madrid

DON BALTAZAR CARLOS ON HORSEBACK
Prado, Madrid

DON BALTAZAR CARLOS AS A HUNTER
Prado, Madrid

THE PRINCESS MARGARITA
Louvre, Paris

THE SURRENDER OF BREDA
Prado, Madrid

PHILIP IV OF SPAIN
Metropolitan Museum of Art, New York

PORTRAIT OF A YOUNG MAN
National Gallery of Art, Washington

DON BALTAZAR CARLOS AND HIS DWARF
Museum of Fine Arts, Boston

SELF PORTRAIT
Metropolitan Museum of Art, New York

VELAZQUEZ, AT THE COURT OF A KING WHO SELDOM SMILED

"Does he never smile?" whispered the Princess Mariana, most apprehensively. "We smile very often at the court of Austria, but here your royal father, the King, has not smiled once that I have seen, and everyone else looks almost as solemn!"

"I can remember his smiling once," nodded Prince Baltazar Carlos decidedly, looking to the Princess Maria Theresa to confirm his statement, "when I caught my first wild boar!"

"It is true," affirmed the Princess just as solemnly. "I well recall that time, and one other, that not so long ago, when his court painter made of him such a true likeness."

Utterly amazed, the young Princess from Austria looked from one to the other. Then she gazed at the high and rather gloomy palace room. It was all so very formal and dignified and somber. It was true that she was used to palace courts and etiquette, but not to rooms which were so dull in color, so heavy in carving, so very high in ceiling that they made her feel very small and so exceedingly dismal. It was more homelike in the court of Austria; there were brighter colors, and not so many queer, stiff rules as these which made up the Spanish court etiquette. The Princess Mariana looked very cross indeed. In the first place, her Spanish dress seemed most uncomfortable with its heavy, wide skirt propped out over hoops, its very tight, uncomfortable waist, its heavy silver braid. One would think she was exceedingly old, she had to move so slowly and so carefully, scarcely able to sit at ease in one of the stiff Spanish chairs with its very tall back and heavy carving. In this gloomy court she was visiting, she would soon forget that she was eleven years old, and would grow to act as if she were five times that age, just as all the others did!

"Why doesn't he smile?" she demanded, tapping her foot impatiently upon the floor. "He would look much more beautiful in his portraits if he did!" Of course she knew that was not a very polite remark for a visiting princess to make. But she was so cross and bored and homesick, she didn't much care! So she gave her very uncomfortable wig—decorated with bows and feathers entwined in its stiff curls—a toss which made it more uncomfortable still, and glanced belligerently around.

"You see, Princess Mariana," patiently explained Don Carlos, sitting up very straight in his heavy black velvet suit, likewise trimmed with silver braid, "our father must look very dignified, for is he not the King of Spain?"

"But kings can smile," argued the Austrian Princess. "Don't you ever get very weary of all the stiff rules of etiquette, Maria Theresa? If I am ever Queen, I shall smile!"

Maria Theresa spread out her wide skirt and played with the big watch which was her delight—a gift sent to her by a prince of France to whom she was betrothed, although she had never seen him. "Yes," she said with a sigh, "I do. Sometimes I wish I were a flower girl on the streets of Madrid; then I could do just as I chose and not be all bound in by so many rules about everything I want to do. When our court painter is making my likeness, I often get him to tell me about sights he has seen."

"And I," added Don Carlos, his eyes beginning to sparkle. "He has seen so many places and so many people, very different from those at our court. He once lived in Seville, where he says the sunlight is brighter than it is here, and when he was just about as old as I, he went into a painter's workshop to learn how to use his colors and his brushes. He says that painter was very cross indeed, much more cross and stern than anyone here at our Spanish court!"

"'Tis hard to believe!" muttered the Austrian Princess rather rudely—but no one heeded.

"Then he studied with a much more pleasant teacher, a scholar, a writer, a poet, as well as a painter," continued Don Carlos, quite undisturbed, "and became betrothed to this master's daughter."

"Just as I am betrothed to you, Don Carlos," courtesied the Princess Mariana, a mischievous look taking the place of the peevish one of a few minutes before. "Diego Velazquez shall paint our portraits together when we are King and Queen!"

The Princess of Spain turned to look at the Princess from the Austrian court. "Then you must remember that you are a Spanish Princess," she told her sternly, "and not play so many jokes at our formal occasions, else Don Carlos will feel very sad indeed. The ladies-in-waiting, Doña Maria and Doña Isabel, have not yet recovered from the shock of seeing those white mice you let loose among them, and the greater shock of feeling them running beneath their long, wide skirts!"

The Princess Mariana giggled. It had sounded so strange to hear them shriek in that somber palace room! Then she made a deep curtsey, as she had seen the ladies of the Spanish court do. "I shall remember!" she mocked, "that at the Court of Spain one must only smile very sedately, and not too often, and laugh not at all!"

"We laugh, though in not too loud a tone," protested Don Carlos. "Do we not, Maria Theresa? You shall see how I laugh when I gallop to the hunt upon my pony, as my father the King, and his minister of affairs, Duke

Olivarez, have taught me. So fast we go that my pony's tail and mane, and my scarf fly to the breeze! One day you shall see us. But come! I have thought of a most wonderful plan to while away the time before we are summoned into the presence of our father. And we must entertain our guest! But no one must know."

Softly he whispered into the ear of his sister, and as cautiously into the very expectant ear of the visiting Princess. Her eyes brightened; so there was some fun at the Spanish court, after all! All bored and peevish expressions disappeared, and as quickly as their long, wide stiff skirts would permit them, they jumped to their feet.

"Follow me!" cried Don Carlos. "I know the way."

Very quietly they crossed the stately, gloomy room, and stood by the heavily paneled wall. Making quite sure that no lady- or gentlemen-in-waiting, no custodian or courtier was anywhere around, the Prince gently touched a panel decorated in curling scrolls and vines. Slowly, very slowly, but surely, the panel moved, slid back and before them appeared a doorway leading into a dim, long, narrow passage.

"Where does it go?" whispered Maria Theresa in a mere breath of a voice. "Come!" urged the Princess Mariana, fearing lest some lady-in-waiting would appear and keep them from their adventure. "That is, if these terrible skirts aren't so wide that we will stick to the walls of this passage!"

"Sh-h!" whispered Don Carlos, "we are just in time. The panel slid back into place just as Doña Maria entered the room searching for us, no doubt to do something we don't want to do!"

"But do you know the way, Don Carlos?" asked Princess Mariana. "I shouldn't want to have to stay here in this dismal passage till someone else happens to touch that panel!"

"Have no fear, Princess Mariana," comforted Maria Theresa. "My father, the King, has many such passages which lead into different parts of the palace, and even if we should lose our way, he would be coming at some time soon!"

Mariana sighed. Everything was queer in this very strange Spanish court, where she was to live one day. She wouldn't want to have to wait in one of these secret passages until the gloomy King of Spain came along!

In silence they walked, each behind the other, the Prince leading the way, until he stopped abruptly, and they could hear him tapping upon the wall before them. Yes, there was a streak of light growing wider and brighter, until they found themselves blinking at the opening leading into a room much lighter than the one they had left.

A man sprang forward, drawing his sword. "Halt! in the name of the King!" he cried.

"Your Majesty!" exclaimed the amazed Mariana.

"It is our father, the King!" gasped Maria Theresa, while Don Carlos gravely bowed before his father, and spoke with a dignity which matched the King's own, "Sire, I saw you one day press the scrolled panel and wondered where the passage led. So I tried it today to see what we should find!"

"Bent on Adventure, I understand," said the King, a pale smile softening his lips, which surprisedly developed into the ghost of a laugh. "I shall have to take care of my secret walks! The next time you wish to traverse this passage, pull the cord just as you enter and the dark curtains will lift to light your way!"

"He really laughed!" whispered the amazed Austrian Princess. "I am so glad that he knows how!"

"Sh-h!" whispered Maria Theresa, aghast. "Our court painter, Diego Rodriguez de Sylva y Velazquez is at work.

We must take care not to disturb him for he is painting the likeness of our father, His Most Sacred Majesty, Philip the Fourth, King of Spain!"

"But I want to see what sort of a court painter he may be," announced the capricious Princess from Austria, "so that I may decide, Don Carlos, whether we shall desire him to paint our portraits!"

The court painter, palette and brushes in hand, had ceased from his work at the sudden appearance of the Royal Children through the secret passage which none but the King, who paid him frequent visits, had ever used before. He smiled. "I hope that I shall please Your Excellencies," he murmured, a twinkle in his eye.

Never before had the rigorous court etiquette been so disturbed. Mariana, actually kept His Most Sacred Majesty, King Philip, waiting! She stood in front of the big canvas and demanded that he explain to her what all the paint there meant!

"Princess Mariana!" cried the shocked Princess of Spain. Don Baltazar Carlos tried to lead her away, but she would not move and it was contrary to court etiquette to drag or pull! "I must request you," began King Philip sternly, no trace of a smile upon his lips. But the court painter Velazquez, never at a loss for just the right words at just the right moment, made a most courtly bow—as well as he could with his palette and brushes to hinder him! "Your Most Gracious Majesty, I can continue my portraits of your most Sacred Self and His Excellency, Duke Olivarez, and at the same time explain the picture to the Princess who honors us with her presence, if it is favorable to your desires."

King Philip again took the pose he had been holding, and slightly nodded his head. Why not? Diego Velazquez' voice always soothed him and the words which he spoke always entertained him. What other king had so wonderful a court painter? He must make him Marshal of the Palace, honor him in many ways. Let him begin his story.

Don Carlos and the Princess Maria Theresa looked at each other in amazement. The Princess Mariana seemed to have no fear of anyone, not even of their father, the King!

"It is a picture of a boar hunt in which the King of Spain and his minister take part, Your Royal Highnesses. These many spectators here in the foreground are watching, even as you are honoring me by doing. Even her Majesty, Queen Isabella, attended by her ladies, is among them, and each is provided with a trident to turn back the boar should he make a mad rush at their royal coaches as he sometimes does. There to your left is His Majesty, the King, and His Excellency, Duke Olivarez, victoriously thrusting a gilded trident into the onrushing wild boar!"

"I have been hunting, too!" cried Don Carlos, "and our illustrious court painter made my likeness upon his canvas with my great hunting dog. I hold a gun, instead of a trident. Have you ever seen a bullfight, Don Diego?"

"Evidently you long to see one," smiled the court painter, keeping on with his picture as he talked, his quick eyes catching what was lacking, and putting just the finishing strokes which were needed to the figure of the King. "Yes, I have been present at a bullfight in Seville. 'Twas on a holiday, and the huge amphitheatre was crowded with thousands of spectators: men wild with excitement as they cheered, women showing their eagerness, too, though 'tis no place for ladies and children of the court. Except, of course, Don Carlos, who may get a glimpse one day," for the court painter had noticed the disappointment beginning to cloud the face of the heir to the Spanish throne. "Now the moment has arrived! Each spectator leans forward, breathless. Into the center of the great ring, the bull plunges, maddened by picadores waving scarlet cloths before his eyes, and there is no color which you can see here upon my palette which the bull hates so much as this warm, bright red. Men throw sharp pointed darts at him pricking his skin, until he is wild with fear and anger. He rushes at the vivid cloth he hates so much—and sometimes catches the man who holds it and tosses him upon his horns. Often the agile picador jumps like lightning to the side, and escapes him. The spectators applaud wildly as each bull is slain. Sometimes the bull is the victor. It is a cruel sport, Your Royal Highnesses, and you would better be spectators, instead, at the next boar hunt of His Majesty, the King."

It was the same Mariana of Austria who came back to Spain a few years later, as Queen, not wedded to Don Baltazar Carlos, to whom she had been betrothed, for the heir to the throne of Spain had died. She came as Queen to King Philip of Spain, the King who so seldom smiled. There were crowds in the narrow streets to watch the magnificent procession and festivities which had been planned by the same court painter, Diego Velazquez, who had been honored by being made Marshal of the Palace, an office of great honor, it is true, but also of much burdensome responsibility. His duty it was to arrange for all the magnificent court festivities, royal hunts, royal journeys and processions and imposing court ceremonies.

Princess Maria Theresa was there to greet the little new Queen, only three years older than herself, and to welcome her once more to the stately, formal Spanish palace. The two Princesses, so near of an age, managed to have some good times in that somber palace, though Queen Mariana, as wife of King Philip, three times as old as she, stiff, somber, and governed by the formal rules of Spanish etiquette, was often very sad.

Thus Velazquez the court painter thought her, as he was painting her portrait one day. "Must you paint me again?" she sighed, standing before him so straight, so stiff, so bored; her waist so tight, her skirt so wide, her hair so frizzed and curled and twisted and tied, a cascade of curls and bows and feathers on each side of her face, that she must have been most uncomfortable. "Why not paint the likeness of our royal daughter, the Infanta Margarita? She, at least, has never been so hindered by Spanish rules of etiquette; her hair does not give her discomfort, and her lips have not forgotten how to curve upward into a smile!"

"Your Majesty," protested the smiling painter, "she will not be still long enough for me to catch her likeness! Although it may be that I have a plan. Come to my studio tomorrow, Your Majesty, together with His Most Sacred Majesty, the King, the Infanta Margarita, her ladies-in-waiting, her dog, her favorite dwarf, whatever and whoever may help to amuse her! I shall paint the picture which will show the Royal Family alive more than any other has done!"

"And which shall give you lasting honor," murmured Queen Mariana. She must remind King Philip that the highest honor was due their court painter who had served them so well.

The great picture was begun. The royal family had gathered in the artist's big, high-ceilinged studio flooded with light. "There, just so!" commanded the eager painter, forgetting that he was speaking to Their Majesties, his royal patrons, and remembering only the great picture he was about to paint. "Behold! I will catch your likeness in yonder mirror! Such has not been done before. Come,

Princess Margarita, stand here, just so, to please your royal parents, who want you to be in the picture with them. See! you shall look right at them and help to make them look pleasant. Now I am getting the soft rose color for your gown, and the silver for its embroidery. That is right, Doña Maria, help keep her still. Her dog may lie just there—the rest of you group yourselves so! Ah! That is right! Curve up your lips, Your Royal Highness, or my brushes will surely imprison your frown! Now, that is better, and while I paint, I shall tell you a story of when I was a boy in Seville."

The little Princess listened, as did the others. The painter worked quickly, telling one story after another as he painted, and also putting into the picture himself at work by his easel, at His Majesty's request. Such depth to the room, such height! Such luminous light and shadow, such reality to the people of the royal court. A glimpse, a visit, to the Royal Family on that day! And the little Princess, so natural, so unspoiled by the Spanish court, that she is like a delicate flower in bloom.

When the picture was finished—and the court painter worked swiftly because of the little Princess who did not like to stand still—Their Majesties stood long before the canvas.

"So we shall always live, Diego Velazquez," murmured the Queen.

"So shall you always be honored, my most worthy court painter," praised His Majesty, the King, and taking one of the artist's brushes, he dipped it in red and painted upon the breast of Diego Velazquez on the canvas, the red cross of Santiago, one of the great Spanish Orders, knighting him—the highest honor he could give his court painter who had served him so well.

REMBRANDT

1606–1669

BEFORE THE STORY

So CLOSELY connected with Holland across the seas are the United States of America that a story of an artist of that land is very near to us. The Dutch settlement of New Amsterdam which today is New York, and the Dutch cities to which the Pilgrim Fathers fled for freedom of worship before they ventured across seas to faraway America, form links of a chain which binds us to the Dutch people who also have always loved Liberty. So much did they love liberty that small Holland bravely fought for its freedom from great and powerful Spain—and won! They had worked hard so many years to save their land from the ever-grasping sea that of course they wanted to have the right to rule themselves. And through their perseverance, their pluck and their courage they won that right and kept it.

There is nothing stiff and formal about the pictures which the Dutch artists made; just everyday scenes and everyday people, so real and so human that you feel you are really in their presence! And they have given us the beauty of their homes, their gardens, their canals, their windmills, and the sturdy, happy people themselves.

The greatest of all these painters was Rembrandt and he is still great throughout his own land and all other lands —Rembrandt van Ryn, or "of the Rhine," because his father's house and mill stood on the banks of the river Rhine. The Master of Light and Shadow, the "King of

Shadows," this artist is often called. Such wonderful portraits he has left us—not only of wealthy Dutch burgomasters, but of the humble folk whose faces, revealing their character formed by suffering as well as by joy, interested him. Especially was he sympathetic with the old, the poor, and the burdened. Always he enables us to see them as he did, not only giving us the feeling they are really before us, but making us acquainted with their personality, their inner selves, until we feel towards them as he did.

Rembrandt was born in 1606 in Leyden, Holland. He was the son of a miller but had no desire to follow his father's business. His mind was made up, even when he was a boy, to become a painter.

He attended the University of Leyden for a time, then went to Amsterdam to study his art and spent much of his life there, painting and teaching.

Some of Rembrandt's Paintings:

PORTRAIT OF AN OLD WOMAN
National Gallery, London
LESSON IN ANATOMY
Ryks Museum, Amsterdam
PORTRAITS OF THE MEMBERS OF THE CLOTH GUILD
Ryks Museum, Amsterdam
SELF PORTRAIT
Metropolitan Museum of Art, New York
OLD WOMAN CUTTING HER NAILS
Metropolitan Museum of Art, New York
SELF-PORTRAIT
National Gallery of Art, Washington
PORTRAIT OF HIMSELF
Frick Collection, New York

FLORA
Metropolitan Museum of Art, New York

THE MASTER OF LIGHT AND SHADOW: REMBRANDT

"It is the University thou must attend, the place where thou wilt learn all that goes to make a good scholar who will bring fame to our city of Leyden," determinedly spoke Rembrandt's father when his son had just turned fourteen. "Here am I, a thrifty miller, working hard at my tasks all the hours of the day to feed the nine children who have come. Be it so! Does not my eldest son, Adriaen, thy brother of whom thou might well take example, plan to follow in his father's steps, as eldest sons should? Have not the others planned to learn trades as soon as their years of schooling are over? Does not even Lijsbeth, thy younger sister, she who is the last one to come to us, follow her mother in learning to care for the house, to sew and embroider, to make good butter and cheese? And thou! What dost thou do, Rembrandt, but draw pictures with thy pencil or brush! Is not the University of our city, which our fathers chose instead of gold, good enough for thee? Speak to that boy of thine, Neeltgen, that he may see wisely as we see!"

Impatiently and yet anxiously Harmen van Ryn left the cheerful, spotless little sitting room where Rembrandt, Lijsbeth, and their mother were seated, stepped into his wooden shoes awaiting him at the door, and went clattering down the narrow brick-paved street along the busy canal, towards his big windmill nearby, the great arms of which were whirling swiftly, helping to grind the corn.

Rembrandt went slowly to the door and looked down the street. Could he, too, like Adriaen, his older brother, learn to like the work in the dusty mill, filling the great sacks with corn and grain, instead of making pictures of the windmills? Or, could he go to the University, and instead of drawing on the pages of his books, study all about the Latin of scholars, and perhaps become a lawyer or a burgomaster? Slowly, he turned back into the room.

It was such a comfortable room. Rembrandt could not help feeling cheered. There sat his mother so that the sunlight direct from the open door and the less bright light which found its way through the red curtains at the high, little window, shone brightly upon her hands busily removing the red coats from a dish of apples. They were such nice hands, such kind hands, Rembrandt thought. He would like to draw them. Suddenly, the bright brass warming pan hanging by the deep fireplace reflected a ray of sunlight, making it glow like red fire. Ah! That was an interesting study of light! There they were, little spots of light dancing upon the bright copper kettles, dishes and candlesticks, until they shone like red-gold! A flash of warm red caught his eye–the tulip plant his sister Lijsbeth was so carefully tending! He had his first glimpse of it in the polished glass of the mirror. "What fun it would be," he thought to himself, "to try to draw a picture of one's own self, seen through the glass of a mirror! One day I shall surely try it. It would be amusing to see how close a likeness one could make of oneself!" "Mother," he asked, drawing nearer to her as she kept her fingers busy at her task, "why is it that Father is so eager for my attendance at the University?"

"Surely, thou dost know that, my son!" replied his mother, reproachfully. "Every boy and girl in Leyden, in all Holland, knows what the University means to the good folk of Leyden."

"I do!" piped Lijsbeth, her plant with its red blossoms still held lovingly in her hands. "Why, Rembrandt, we have had that story told us often in the school!"

Rembrandt looked expectantly at his mother and at Lijsbeth on the other side of her, the light falling full upon her broad white collar, and her little, close-fitting white cap. Quite unconsciously, Rembrandt's fingers began to busy themselves with the scrap of paper and the pencil he had brought forth from his jacket. A white cap framing a face, and a broad white collar to reflect the light would look well in a picture. In Rembrandt's mind formed a picture which one day he was going to paint of his sister, Lijsbeth, her face and cap in the full light which he would like so much to know how to make. Even as his fingers made their quick, sure strokes, his ears were taking in every word his mother was saying. And well Vrouw van Ryn knew it; of all her family of children none liked better to hear a story, whether it were Bible, history, or fairy tale, than her youngest son, Rembrandt.

"Over forty years ago," began the mother, her fingers still busy with the rosy apples, "the Spanish people ruled our land. King Philip of Spain and his general were cruel masters who thought their people lived but for the use and pleasure of those in power, instead of the rulers living and working for the good of their people. When we of Holland, who have always loved freedom, could stand it no longer, Prince William the Silent, so-called because he was a man of few words, knowing well how to keep his counsel, came to our aid. Leyden, this very city in which we live, was held in siege by a Spanish general. Food grew very scarce and all the people suffered. 'Let the brave folk of Leyden hold out for three months' time for the sake of all Holland!' Prince William begged. Mark ye well that our city had no trained soldiers then except the small City Guard."

"But so brave were those few men, the schoolmaster said," declared Lijsbeth, "that they were worth twice ten thousand Spanish men!"

Rembrandt said no word, but his fingers had ceased their sketching. He was seeing pictures with his mind-eyes, a very faraway, dreamy look upon his face. Well did his mother know that look; it meant that he would soon be absorbed in the making of another picture. Only his eyes, which now never left her face, begged her to go on.

"Days went dragging by. Each day the heroes watched from the tower for their only hope, the Dutch ships which did not come, though by our Prince's order the dikes were pierced and the waters flowed in swiftly from the sea. Each dike within the land was held by the Spanish foe, and an east wind drove the rescuing ships back. There was no meat, no bread. No blade of grass was left by the starving people, and each day they watched in vain for the ships which could not come. Most of the brave Leydeners had no thought of surrender. Upon them depended for freedom not only Leyden but all Holland."

"Did not some beg to surrender?" breathed Rembrandt, remembering what he had heard before of that famous siege.

"Some few, my son, who were worn out, weakened, starving, reproached the heroic burgomaster who had promised Prince William not to surrender and who was determined to keep his word. 'Accept the Spanish terms of surrender!' they pleaded. 'Better that, than dying of starvation!' 'Surrender, do you ask?' cried Burgomaster van der Werf. 'I have pledged myself to Prince William to hold this city. Starvation is better than dishonor. Take my body to appease your hunger, but expect no surrender as long as I remain alive.' "

"And they waited!" exulted Lijsbeth, jumping up so quickly in her excitement that she almost upset her tulip plant.

"Until a great storm came," remembered Rembrandt, his eyes sparkling. "It swept far inland with the changing wind, and the waters hurried through the broken dikes, and the Dutch ships appeared to save them!"

"With food for the poor starving mothers and fathers and boys and girls. Can you not just see them stretching out their thin arms after so many weeks of suffering?" asked tenderhearted Lijsbeth. "Were they not the bravest people in Holland, my mother, to send away those wicked Spanish tyrants? And such a little country, too, to win its freedom."

"Sometimes little countries overcome the great, because 'Right makes Might,' so my schoolmaster says," offered Rembrandt sagely. "But thou hast not told us, Mother, what the bravery of those who lived in Leyden just before us, has to do with the University the good father wishes me to attend?"

"Prince William was so proud of the brave Leyden folk for their resistance against the Spanish siege, that as a reward he gave them the choice between freedom from taxes and the building of this University and the people of the city met and . . ."

"They chose the University! I know!" cried Lijsbeth in high glee, vigorously clapping her hands. "I should think that any boy would be proud to go there."

Rembrandt did not answer. It was so hopeless to try to make them see. Though his good mother did almost always understand. She knew that he would like to do as his father wished. But he knew that by doing so he would not bring honor or fame to Leyden as his father thought. Were not artists needed as well as lawyers and burgomasters? Artists, who could make Leyden, even all Holland with its people and houses, its canals and its great windmills, live for all those coming after them to enjoy?

"Come!" whispered Rembrandt to Lijsbeth after her work in helping her mother was done. "I will show thee a very wonderful thing I have found!"

Lijsbeth was always very glad to go with this brother, next to her in age, and so different from her older brothers, who were always too busy to bother with her at all. Whereas her brother Rembrandt never seemed to mind when she sat quietly by his side and watched him at the making of his pictures. Sometimes, he told her stories about them as he worked. Often, they begged their mother for Bible stories, and then Rembrandt would make pictures of them, so real that they told the story without words. But never before had he taken her with him on a visit to their father's mill.

"Art thou going to turn miller like our father and our brother Adriaen?" she asked very softly, as they tiptoed past the millers piling up their great sacks of corn, the light from the lantern shining upon their faces and broad shoulders, the rest of the room in shadow. So quietly did they go, and so busy were the millers at their work, that Rembrandt and Lijsbeth, quite unnoticed, crept to a little room above, where the pale light was straggling in through one small window.

"Watch!" whispered Rembrandt. Curiously, Lijsbeth's gaze followed his. What could be the wonderful thing her brother had found? Brighter grew the sun's rays, a few of the more adventuresome ones bursting in a golden glow into the dark little room. Some of them caressed the wondering face of Lijsbeth.

"Was that not wonderful, my sister?" asked Rembrandt in great glee. "All the rest of this room was in shadow, but so clearly couldst thou be seen in the sunlight, every expression on thy face, every one of the hairs of thy head like a thread of gold! That is what I am going to learn to do—paint shadow, and sunlight shining upon a face, a hand, a snowy collar and cap! And mark thee, Lijsbeth, I shall thus do more for Leyden and Holland than if I became a miller, a sailor, or attended the University and grew into a learned burgomaster. Thou, and our mother and father, the great men of our cities, the soldiers—all shall live through my pictures. That I promise thee! And my tools shall be color and light and shadow. One day our father will be glad, and our mother, too. I think she has for many days known and been glad that I would become a painter of pictures."

Amsterdam was a beautiful city—like Venice, formed of many islands, with streets of water crossed by hundreds of bridges. To that city with its many, steep, gabled houses, its high-steepled churches, its harbors of foreign-looking ships, Rembrandt went to live, after he had studied under artists in Leyden, and after he himself had become a painter of pictures. Then he returned to his smaller home city, where he had lived as a boy. There he studied each day by himself.

"Nature shall be my master," he decided. "Have I not the sun's rays which give light in Leyden as well as in Amsterdam? Am I not rich in subjects? Have I not my brothers and sister to sit for me? And my mother? Where could I ever find a subject more patient, more beautiful, with her kindly face? There are the Bible stories which

I can put upon canvas. And have I not my own face which will smile, or frown, or look very solemn at my will?" He spent some years in making these real-looking potraits, as well as the pictures which came to his mind.

But to Amsterdam he went to live in his twenty-fifth year, for to that city flocked many artists; there he could see fine pictures. To Amsterdam the Dutch merchants brought in their ships many beautiful things.

" 'Tis a good place to be," one of his pupils would murmur, after a hard day's work studying from the master, trying in vain to capture his skill in making a portrait look like true flesh and blood, the flesh fairly glowing in light and looking as " 'twould feel to the fingers." He stretched himself at ease in one of the little rooms which Rembrandt had fitted up for his pupils in the attic of his gabled house.

"Only today I sold a picture designed after one of his," offered another. "And where else should we see such beautiful things? Such treasures brought back from the East in our Dutch ships! Swords and daggers with jeweled patterns! Furs, rugs, and corals strange to the eye! Velvet-pink shells from no one knows what faraway isle! And such costumes, velvets and silks, in which to dress up for one's portrait!"

" 'Twas but the other day," laughed another of the pupils, "that I saw our master in the armor of some grand dignitary or knight, looking so intently at himself in that long mirror downstairs in the room with the high window which he uses for the study of light breaking through the shadows. First he smiled! Then he laughed! He looked sad, he frowned, then, very stern and soldierly, and so he painted himself!"

"For all his study of light and of shadow and his fondness for dressing up himself and his subjects, yet no one

Saint Francis Preaching to the Birds

ATTRIBUTED TO GIOTTO

Upper Church of St. Francis, Assisi

Madonna, Child and Two Angels

BY FRA FILIPPO LIPPI

Uffizi Gallery, Florence

The Madonna of the Rocks

BY LEONARDO DA VINCI

The Louvre, Paris

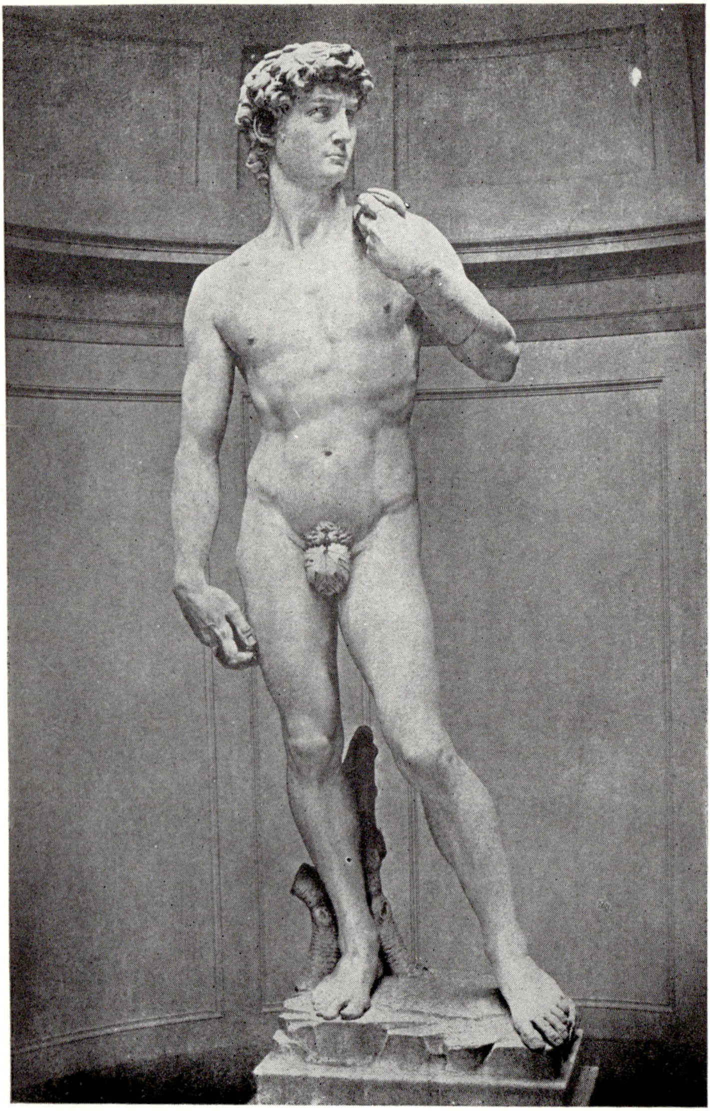

David

BY MICHELANGELO

The Academy, Florence

Madonna, Child and Little Saint John
(known as "The Madonna of the Chair")

BY RAPHAEL

The Pitti Art Gallery, Florence

Saint George and the Dragon

BY RAPHAEL

The National Gallery, Washington

Madonna, Child and Little Saint John
(known as "The Madonna of the Chair")

BY RAPHAEL

The Pitti Art Gallery, Florence

Saint George and the Dragon

BY RAPHAEL

The National Gallery, Washington

Courtesy of the Metropolitan Museum of Art, New York

A View of Toledo

BY EL GRECO

Metropolitan Museum of Art, New York

Rubens' Two Sons, Albert and Nicolas

BY PETER PAUL RUBENS

Liechtenstein Gallery, Vienna

The Musician

BY FRANS HALS

The Ryks Museum, Amsterdam
(After the original in the possession of
Baron Robert de Rothschild, Paris)

The Children of Charles I of England:
Charles, Mary and James

BY SIR ANTHONY VAN DYCK

Picture Gallery, Turin

The Maids of Honor

BY VELAZQUEZ

The Prado Museum, Madrid

Courtesy Brown-Robertson Co., Inc., New York

The Night Watch, or The Company of Captain Frans Banning Co

BY REMBRANDT VAN RYN

The Ryks Museum, Amsterdam

Courtesy of the Metropolitan Museum of Art, New York

Young Girl With a Water Jug

BY JOHANNES VERMEER

Metropolitan Museum of Art, New York

Courtesy of the Metropolitan Museum of Art, New York

Georgiana Augusta Frederica Seymour

BY SIR JOSHUA REYNOLDS

Metropolitan Museum of Art, New York

Courtesy Brown-Robertson Co., Inc., New York

The Blue Boy—Portrait of Jonathan Buttall

BY THOMAS GAINSBOROUGH

Henry E. Huntington Library and Art Gallery, San Marino, California

Courtesy of the Metropolitan Museum of Art, New York

George Washington

BY GILBERT STUART

Metropolitan Museum of Art, New York

Courtesy of the Metropolitan Museum of Art, New York

A Path Through the Trees

BY COROT

Metropolitan Museum of Art, New York

The Gleaners

BY JEAN FRANÇOIS MILLET

The Louvre, Paris

Courtesy Museum of Fine Arts, Boston

Fog Warning (*also known as "Halibut Fishing"*)

BY WINSLOW HOMER

Museum of Fine Arts, Boston

Portrait of the Artist's Mother:
Arrangement in Grey and Black

BY WHISTLER

The Louvre, Paris

From a Copley Print, © by Curtis and Cameron, Boston

Galahad the Deliverer
(from "The Quest of The Holy Grail")
Public Library, Boston

BY EDWIN AUSTIN ABBEY

knows better than he the anatomy of the human form," remarked one. "That is how I happened to become his pupil."

"Many great people of Amsterdam have commissioned him to paint their portraits," remarked the one who had first spoken, "but in truth I believe that he likes best of all to paint the portrait of some old lady with wrinkled face framed by her white cap, and surrounded by her ruffled white collar; or some grandfather with his wrinkled, gnarled hands. Far better, he likes to picture them than fashionable ladies and important burgomasters! No doubt it is because his whole heart is in his task of making flesh like real flesh, glowing in the light; the play of light and of shadow in every wrinkle."

"I was well fooled one day," laughed the youngest of the pupils, making a wry face. " 'Twas soon after Vrouw Saskia came as the master's wife. Coming in from a ride down the canal at noonday, I swear that I thought them there before me beside the table, she in a blue robe and velvet bodice sitting upon the master's knee and smiling at me; he, in a dark red coat and black velvet hat with soft white feathers curling around it, and holding up a sparkling glass! So real did they look, in color and light and expression as the light struck the picture the master had just finished, that I spoke to them. Mynheer Rembrandt had stolen in behind me and how he laughed! But he was pleased that I mistook his picture for life. He is a great painter with a ready eye and a fine understanding of people." The others nodded. "All Holland will be proud of him."

Eight happy and prosperous years brought Rembrandt commissions for many pictures from cities all over Holland. Then Vrouw Saskia sickened and died, leaving him with a nine-months-old baby boy, named Titus. Even his interest in the great group picture he had been commissioned to paint, had waned. For had not the men who had asked him to paint it shown their disappointment and displeasure?

Even the children upon the street talked about the painting of the company of soldiers.

"My father is the captain!" boasted one whose father was Frans Banning Cocq, captain of the company of soldiers, who were pictured in the act of being summoned out from the meeting hall of the civic guard. "His picture is in the very front, and my father says it is a very fine painting and that the painter is a very great man. He made my father look just as real, and the light is shining on the golden undersleeves of his black coat and on his white collar, which my mother had pleated and starched until it was 'a work of art,' she said. And thou canst see the bright crimson of his scarf all trimmed with figures of gold!"

"And my father, too!" interrupted another, who had several times attempted to speak. "My father is the lieutenant and my mother says she is very proud of the way he looks in that picture, right by the captain's side. The light shines on his golden yellow coat and hat and white sash. I wanted to put out my finger and touch the feather in my father's hat when I went to see the picture with him, it looked so soft and real. My! he is standing in such a bright light that everyone can see him! My father says that all the talk in Amsterdam against Mynheer Rembrandt van Ryn is very wrong; that he is a wonderful artist!"

"But my father can't be seen!" shouted another excitedly. "Just one side of his face! And he is just as good a soldier and paid just as much for his portrait as thy father! He asked my good mother, 'Is it right?' And she said, 'My Jan deserves to be remembered as well as Captain Frans and his lieutenant, who take up the front of the picture and all the light!' "

"Even so," muttered another, "look at my father! Just part of his head and his arm, scarce showing at the side. First dost thou see his big drum, and then dost thou see just a part of his head, as if he were playing at peekaboo like our small Katrina! Has he not paid to the artist his guldens to have his portrait painted? Nay, this Rembrandt, he is a queer one! It is Mynheer Frans Hals who knows how to paint groups of people to hang in our halls. Through him the members of the civic guard would have had equal attention to their portraits, not some so far in the background and so much in the darkness that they can scarcely be seen!"

"Their money's worth!" groaned the great artist, Rembrandt, as he crossed to stand in front of his masterpiece in its place in the hall of the company of soldiers he had undertaken to paint. "Is that all they think of in a painting? Do they care naught for the beauty of light and of shadow? The illumination of the faces? What complaint have they? Though many of the bodies are in shadow, are not the sixteen faces almost all in the light? And is not a face and its expression of more worth than a body? Do they care not for my problem in grouping? Never will I sacrifice my art to the whims of my patrons and place each of the group in a stiff, straight row, each equally important in position. What care I took in painting the little girl to balance the figure of the gallant lieutenant on the right of the captain! The expression of the hands, their modeling to imitate muscles, bones, and yielding flesh! The shadow of the captain's hand upon the lieutenant's yellow coat; the placing of the long lances, catching the light, the blue and red banners; the rest and the motion;

the patterns of hats and helmets merging into the shadowy ground; even the sound of the drum! Do all these mean nothing? The depth I have tried for, and the rich golden glow over it all?"

Sadly the painter shook his head. "Alas, for those who care not for the painter's art! Such fickle folk with minds which do not understand. If only my mother, who always believed in the pictures I longed to make, were with me; my Saskia, who so helped me in my work. Little Titus, thou shalt inspire me to keep on at the painting of pictures! An artist must never forsake his art. But only the few understand, like the good Jan Six, who will one day be burgomaster of our city, and who has promised that I shall be chosen to paint his portrait. He knows it is the idea and the soul of the picture the artist of vision must strive for, not just the outside form. I must comfort myself with the thought that though the people of Holland today have not the eyes to see and the hearts to understand, the people in after years will—eh, my small Titus?"

JOHANNES VERMEER

(Known as Jan Vermeer van Delft)

1632–1675

BEFORE THE STORY

Who has not longed to visit Holland, that picturesque, fascinating country where the very windmills seem to be waving their arms in welcome, where many old customs and costumes may still be enjoyed, where there are streets of water with protecting banks or dikes, and where fishing boats bring their catch, and trading boats their treasures? Who has not longed to glide lazily in a bright-sailed boat down one of the canals, or skate upon it when it is frozen in winter?

Red and orange sails fill with the breeze, wingèd caps frame happy faces, wooden shoes clatter down the cobbled streets, wind-swept clouds race across the sky from which the sun peeps out to shine down upon gay beds of hyacinths, narcissus, and tulips. Many fields of these colorful blossoms brighten Holland.

Such a brave little country Holland has always been, winning for itself the name of "The Land of Pluck." A small country it is, low-lying, with no hills and mountains, but flat, wet land as its name tells us. Does it not seem strange that the land is lower than the sea? Yet the water does not overflow it because of the great walls of stone and earth, called dikes. They are high and wide, so wide that people walk upon them and even carts are driven on the top. Without these protecting dikes to keep back Holland's enemy, the sea, many lives would be lost.

How the Dutch people love their yellow-green fields, the broad sweep of cloud-patterned sky, the shade trees along the canals, the busy windmills, the shining gabled houses with their red and yellow tulips sparkling in the sunlight, the harbor filled with high masts and colored sails, and treasure ships, well laden.

Most of the big countries surrounding Holland have tried to control it at one time or another, but the plucky Dutch folk were determined to be their own masters and rule the land they had protected from the sea with so much patience, skill, and bravery. They were willing to give up anything to save their country. The people of Leyden even went without food until they were nearly starved, to endure a siege by the enemy. To drive away the Spanish foe, they even pierced their dike to let the water into the land so that the Dutch ships might come to help them.

How proud of their hard-won independence they were in the seventeenth century, the century when the Pilgrims came to these shores. The Dutch were determined to show the whole world how thrifty and rich small Holland was. More and more treasures found their way to the Dutch shores through merchants who ventured into many distant ports: Persian rugs, blue and white Chinese porcelain jars, pagoda-figured Chinese wall paper—all became very popular in Holland and also found their way to neighboring countries, and finally to America across the seas.

Do you wonder that the Dutch artists of the seventeenth century were eager to picture their brave, picturesque little country? Do you wonder that they told in their pictures all about their fellow countrymen out-of-doors and inside their very clean, glowing little houses? Their canals, their fields, their tulip beds, their windmills silhouetted against the wind-swept sky, the boys and girls skating up and down the frozen waterways—all appear in their pictures, revealing beauty in the most commonplace everyday things. We of today may enjoy it with them and feel acquainted with the Dutch folk, big and small, and with their homes and country just as they meant us to do. They did not make religious, historical, or court pictures, as often as everyday pictures of their homes and their people, among them, portraits of members of the Civic Guards, Burgomasters and their wives, shipbuilders, merchants, fishermen, grandparents, mothers and fathers, boys and girls. Robert Browning says:

> "We're made so that we love
> First when we see them painted, things we have passed
> Perhaps a hundred times, nor cared to see."

One of these artists who left us such beautiful pictures of Dutch homes filled with a sparkling, vibrant light, is Johannes Vermeer, commonly called Jan Vermeer. Examine his "Young Woman with a Water Jug," which you will find among the illustrations in this book. See how he makes the light shine through a large window, sparkle upon the wall, the map, and the Dutch girl who, in her white cap and broad collar, yellow and blue jacket and rich blue skirt, makes a delightful pattern as she stands against the lighter background. The lower roller of the map is like a finger pointing to her, just as the painter meant it to be. How delightful the color pattern is, especially the rich, clear, sparkling blue. How strong an appeal to the sense of touch in the bronze pitcher and basin, and the heavy rug brought in a Dutch ship from an Eastern port and used by the Dutch housewife as a table covering.

At once we can see that Jan Vermeer was very much more interested in light and color pattern than in anything else. "The Perfect Painter," he was often called, the "Master of the Brush and Palette." How altogether charming is the "Pearl Necklace," not so much because of the lady in azure blue and pale gold who holds out the pearl necklace to catch the glow of light, as because of a dazzling white wall behind her giving plenty of space for the luminous light! How pleasing are his color harmonies, pearl-gray, blue, and lemon-yellow, cooler color harmonies and light than the warmer ones of his fellow-artist, Pieter de Hooch.

We must become acquainted with Vermeer through the sunny windows of his delightful pictures since we know so little of his life, for he, the Painter of Light, is the least known of the great painters of Holland. But here we are in Delft, one of the most quaint and picturesque towns of Holland.

Some of Johannes Vermeer's Pictures:

A VIEW OF DELFT FROM THE ROTTERDAM CANAL
Royal Picture Gallery, The Hague
THE LACE MAKER
Louvre, Paris
A MAIDSERVANT POURING OUT MILK
Ryks Museum, Amsterdam
PORTRAIT OF A YOUNG GIRL
Royal Picture Gallery, The Hague
A YOUNG LADY SEATED AT THE SPINET
National Gallery, London
WOMAN WEIGHING GOLD
National Gallery of Art, Washington
THE SMILING GIRL
National Gallery of Art, Washington

A Girl Asleep
Metropolitan Museum of Art, New York
Officer and Laughing Girl
Frick Collection, New York
The Concert
Isabella Stewart Gardner Museum, Boston

THROUGH SUNNY DUTCH WINDOWS: JOHANNES VERMEER

"You'll like the Master," confided young Pieter, nodding convincingly. "Why, Master Fabritius has been to Amsterdam, and studied with the great Master Rembrandt. Yes, it is so! Fortunate we are indeed to have such a master. That's what I say!"

"You are right, Pieter. We are fortunate to have a master who has been a pupil of the great Rembrandt van Ryn. Everyone in Amsterdam wants a portrait painted by him—burgomasters, shipbuilders, members of the guilds and syndics, soldiers, mothers, fathers, and the old folk, too, with whom he has especial sympathy."

"And no wonder, Jan! He is a wizard and sees not only the eyes and nose and mouth, the shape of the head and color of the hair, but the very soul!"

Jan nodded. "And his understanding of light! Master Fabritius says that his painting of the members of the Civic Guard of Amsterdam is flooded with a wonderful, golden light, which merges into rich, deep shadows."

"Master Fabritius says," laughed Pieter, "that the members of the company not as clearly seen as Captain Frans Banning Cocq and his officer, who are drenched with light in the foreground of the picture, bitterly complained.

Disappointed they were, and their families, too, that they could not be clearly seen. Each wanted his face to show well. Each had paid his money. Our master says that the great Rembrandt was discouraged, but unwilling to sacrifice his art, his beauty of light and shadow, that each face might be seen equally!"

"Yet you can understand how the soldiers felt, Pieter. It hurt their pride to be thrust back into the shadows. If they paid their money they wanted to be seen. Besides, they had boasted of their pictures to their families —and then to find themselves out of the light! He pleased his sitters much better in his portraits for the Cloth Makers' Guild in Amsterdam—or so 'tis rumored. Everyone could be seen, and yet the grouping is natural and effective, and the pattern of color and light and dark very lovely. They seem intent upon someone at the other side of the room and one of them is in the act of rising from the chair. It is so lifelike that they seem about to move and speak, and the table covering is a masterpiece in its appeal to the sense of touch."

" 'Tis rumored that Mynheer Rembrandt paints portraits so real that they have been mistaken for life, greatly to his delight. And how often he paints his own portrait, standing before a mirror and studying each changing expression. Mynheer Fabritius says that one day he entered the room unheard, and there was Rembrandt posed before his mirror, laughing aloud, and painting himself with sure, swift strokes, taking delight in the play of light and shadow in every wrinkle! Sometimes he frowns, sometimes he looks sad, angry, or frightened. He studies each expression and quickly captures it upon canvas. I suppose he feels that he can be more patient in his pose than another."

"Often he dons a velvet cape and hat, and thus paints

himself as a nobleman's son; or gets into a breastplate and gorget and paints himself as a knight. He is said to engrave as rapidly and wonderfully as he paints."

"Jan, I'm going to try to take my mother to Amsterdam that the great Rembrandt may capture her likeness as she sits before him in her very best gown and spotless collar and cuffs. In no way do I want to offend our master, Mynheer Fabritius, for he paints fine portraits and lucky we are, as you have said, to have him to teach us. But my mother is going to have the very best!"

"I'd feel just as you do, Pieter, if I wanted to have a portrait painted, but what I want is sunlight! I want to learn to paint wide open windows drenched with sparkling sunlight, not the golden glow you love and I hear the great Rembrandt uses, but a cooler, more sparkling light, a regular poem of light. You shall see."

But Pieter was hard at work and had quite forgotten Jan, which was just as well, for both were very busy and the light would soon be gone.

The workshop of Karel Fabritius, who had studied under the great Rembrandt in Amsterdam, was a popular one in Delft and there was always plenty going on. When Jan had entered as apprentice boy, he had been at once set to work grinding colors, cleaning and "setting" palettes or stone tables which the Dutch artists often used instead, stretching canvases, learning most of all from watching the master. Then came the long awaited permission to copy one of the master's pictures. Jan had gone beyond that stage in his training and was busy painting a composition of his own.

"Study my pictures, Jan," the master would counsel him, "and those of other painters, but never be a slave to another's manner. Develop your own style, plan your own compositions, arrange your own color harmonies. Be original in your picture making, lad, and you will go far."

Jan, a black velvet cap set well back on his rather long hair, was often hard at work in Fabritius' studio in Delft, which was a large comfortable room with plenty of light. He was remembering his master's counsel, as he set to work upon the canvas before him. He glanced around the familiar studio room, almost as if he were seeing it all with a new vision. There was the map on the wall that under the master's direction he had been allowed to paint with quaint little pictures of Dutch towns and ships in the border. Jan Vermeer smiled. What fun it had been to paint them!

He looked at the beautiful tapestry hanging at his left, and could experience its "feel" with his eyes almost as well as with his hands. Yes, he must put in his pictures just such beautiful hangings and Eastern rugs which Dutch traders had brought back in their ships from far Eastern ports and made popular among the housewives of Holland. They gave a splendid chance for color patterns as well as for texture, or appeal to the sense of touch through the eyes. Chairs with their velvet seats, their thick fringes and brass bosses would break wall spaces well. He'd try a composition that very afternoon, and he'd make the fringes look so real that Karel Fabritius himself would find his fingers itching to run through them.

"I'll paint things as I see them," he declared for the benefit of his good friend, Pieter, and the other boys and young men in the studio, "and I'll try to make others see them as I do, and feel the same joy that always goes leaping through me when I look at any interesting pattern of light and dark masses, of beautiful colors, or sparkling, clear light. Just look at the flood of light coming through yonder window, making even the chandelier, ugly enough in itself, quite a fascinating study. And color!

'Twould take a lifetime to get each color value right. Our Master Fabritius follows the great Rembrandt, with whom he has studied, and uses warm luminous tone, a rich golden light enveloped in shadows. He is so young, Pieter, only a few years older than we, that sometimes I nearly forget that I am his pupil and must say 'Master, this!' and 'Master, that!' Often I feel like calling him 'Karel'!"

"What kind of light did you say you were going to paint in your picture, friend Jan?" asked Pieter, steadily working away at the copy which had been set him.

"Like that flooding the walls and the map—clear, cool, sparkling, almost dancing light! And color! Ah, Pieter, you will one day see how I shall combine lovely clear yellows, regular canary yellows, and rich blues, pearl-grays and of course, blacks and whites to give accent or tone. I shall blend them so that they will happily balance one another, and perhaps place a small bright spot of red in just the right place to complete the color harmony, like a bouquet of colorful flowers! Which color do I like best? I think that it must be blue, for I seem to want to use it most."

"That's because you live in Delft," laughed another young pupil, "have visited the potters' shops so many times, and even painted the lovely blue and white decorations patterned after the Chinese porcelains. Might that not be so?"

"It might," admitted Jan, leaning back in his chair to rest from his work. "Those color patterns of blue in relation to white are beautiful in decoration. My head is full of the pictures I am going to make! When I look at a fresh piece of canvas, I always see a picture taking form upon it full of light and color. One day I am going to paint a girl standing near an open casement window, and her yellow jacket shall have blue trimming and her skirt shall be rich, though soft blue, like the one the master's wife wore yesterday. The sparkling sunlight will shine upon the wall and map, upon the maiden's kerchief and cap, casting many reflected lights upon the brass pitcher she is holding by the handle, and upon the basin on the table, and on the heavy covering bringing out the color pattern. Can you seem to see it, Pieter?"

"Can I see it, Jan? As you tell of it I can see it finished—almost, but not quite! Can you see another picture already planned in your mind?"

"That I can, Pieter, many of them just waiting to come to life. I see another room, its white wall light-drenched, clear and bright, from another window. A girl stands there bathed in that light, admiring before a mirror her necklace of pearls, each pearl a drop of almost magic light. Here are more which often come to my mind: a lady writing at a table; bringing music from a spinet; one of our cobbled Delft streets backed by gabled, brick houses; children playing in a courtyard; a maiden in a yellow bodice leaning forward weaving delicate lace on a blue pillow, the wall behind her a pearl gray. And so I could go on dreaming pictures, Pieter. But now to make these dream pictures really come true! That's my problem."

Many of them he did create upon his canvases when he was a painter in his own right, was even elected a master of the famous Delft Guild of St. Luke. He painted pictures which today are the delight of all who see them, simple pictures, all of them, but deep thought and hard work and clear purpose lay behind them.

"Come, my Martha," he urged one bright morning when the sun and clear sea air made the gabled houses and cobbled streets of Delft even more clear and bright and shining. "You shall be my model today. Is it not an honor that your painter-father wants to capture your likeness for all to see?"

"I, a model, my father? Take Catarina, now, our maidservant. She has beauty which I have not."

"Beauty, Martha? You have color in your cheeks, have you not? Color in your eyes, and on your lips? A pleasing color pattern in your blue turban and its scarf of blue and yellow, and your dress of yellow-green? Is there not beauty in all that, Martha? And in the play of light and shadow which I see now around your head as you look at me over your shoulder? Keep that pose, just so. To keep you quiet and that look of interest in your eyes, I will talk to you."

"About Holland, Father, and the way it won independence from the Spanish foe. Each one of us has been asked to tell of it in our class at school."

The moments passed swiftly, Jan Vermeer intent upon his palette, his brushes, the picture growing upon his canvas, his daughter holding her pose as she listened to her father's story of the plucky, brave little country in which they lived.

"And so, Martha, the brave Dutch folk won their independence of which we are justly proud," her father concluded. "Spain found that power and might could not always win, but that with the aid of all the plucky, brave people and of Almighty God, our Dutch leaders under William of Orange, who loved true liberty, made justice and right conquer. Every new injustice and outrage on the part of the Spanish foe made our people more brave and more determined to be free.

"You know how the staunch folk of Leyden held out when they were besieged, even though they were starving, and finally pierced their dikes that the sea might bring the Dutch ships to their aid. The people of Haarlem were just as brave. 'To get into Holland, we must seize Haarlem, the key to all the Dutch country,' declared the Spanish leaders. 'It will be an easy task.' "

"How stupid those old Spaniards were," Martha cried. "Little did they know the people of our land!"

"Just so, Martha. But suppose you hold your pose—and your tongue—that I may paint your portrait!

"The Spanish foe knew that the walls of Haarlem were weak, the garrison numbering only a few thousand against their thirty thousand trained troops. But they did not reckon with the unconquerable spirit of the people of our land which we wrested from the sea! Just as in Leyden, each one in Haarlem—men, women, and children—did his part, working night and day to defend his town. Never had the Spanish troops met with such a determined and fierce resistance.

"The Spaniards laid siege to Haarlem. Food grew scarce even as it did in Leyden. Our people outside the city tried to help those within, but the Spaniards were always on the watch. Winter changed to Spring and still the siege held, and the folk of Haarlem were perishing from hunger. Better to endure famine than the rule of the Spanish foe, was the decision of each one.

"At last, the discouraged Spaniards offered them terms which they could honorably meet, but which were not kept by the faithless foe, costing the lives of two thousand of Haarlem's brave defenders. It was a costly victory for the besiegers, however, for they lost twelve thousand men!

"The Spaniards might be strong on land, but the Dutch won victory after victory on the sea. Just picture the scene, Martha, when the brave defenders of Leyden pierced their dikes, and at last the wind changed, sent the huge waves far over the land, and the Dutch ships upon their crests, over the ruined dikes, even over the roofs of the houses, straight towards the terrified foe in their besieging forts! Leyden was saved from its foe. The wind changed again, the waves went rushing back into the sea, and the brave Leydeners began to repair their broken dikes. Martha, we live in a wonderful land, filled with very plucky and enduring people."

Martha nodded, thoughtfully, and decided that the siege of Leyden and of Haarlem should be the subject of the history story she must get ready for her class in school, thinking also that were she an artist she would paint the Dutch warships entering the harbor as some of the Dutch artists already had. She would thus help folk remember the bravery of the Dutch heroes.

"See, Martha, what a good model you have been! I have captured the look of interest upon your face, the blue of your headdress and gown, the light around your head, the reflection of it on the pendant in your ear. Here you are in this 'Portrait of a Young Girl,' as I shall call it. Rest now, but tomorrow you shall sit for me again that I may perfect the modeling of your face in light and shadow, the blue and yellow and the light upon them. What is the use of a painter having wife and children if he cannot make use of them!"

"It's Geritje's turn for the next picture," Martha made haste to declare when her pose was ended. "You should paint her, or Catarina as she looked the other day standing at the kitchen table pouring milk from a jug into a bowl. The table was filled with a number of other things such as a basket filled with bread, a pitcher, and some vegetables scattered about. But the light from that high window to the left gave them all a very real beauty, Father, and Catarina looked so lovely in it, too. Would that be too simple and too humble in its setting?"

"Nothing is too simple, or too humble, Martha. That

is a great truth, and we Dutch have been among the first to know the beauty of the most simple everyday things. There—I have made a note of your suggestion. I'll have Geritje or Catarina take that pose of which you speak, and we will call the picture, 'A Maidservant Pouring Out Milk.' And when people look upon it and see the beauty in it, they will realize the truth of seeing beauty in the most humble things—so long as they have lovely form, light and shadow, and color pleasing to the eye. Look, Martha, in the other room! There stands your mother by the window reading a letter which she is holding in the light. The table with its covering, the book upon it, the map upon the wall with the light falling on them both, the chairs, all make a fine arrangement of light and dark. See how her blue silk jacket picks up the light and holds it, and the way the light floods the wall. I'll fill the picture with light—clear and sparkling, radiant light!"

GAINSBOROUGH AND REYNOLDS

Gainsborough 1727–1788
Reynolds 1723–1792

BEFORE THE STORY

Pictures, pictures, everywhere! On the walls of our homes, in our books and magazines and papers, until we are so used to enjoying them that we sometimes do not give enough thought to how they came into being. For of course they all have stories connected with them, of how they came to be painted or carved or drawn, stories which have to do with the lives of the artists who created them.

We are familiar with the picture of the Blue Boy, for instance, but do we know the man who pictured it in his mind and then upon his canvas; whose fingers obeyed the message they received, and fashioned the picture which only the artist had seen perfected in his imagination? Thomas Gainsborough—a good sounding name for an artist or for any man! But where did he live, and when? Did he go to school when he was a boy, play games? How did he look? Was he a real, human person? These are some of the questions that we ask ourselves.

So, let me introduce you now to this artist of England who was born over two hundred years ago—in 1727.

Really, I am introducing two great makers of English pictures, the other being Sir Joshua Reynolds, born in England in 1723, who is said to have also had something to do with calling the Blue Boy into being!

Joshua Reynolds, the older of these two artists, was a native of Plympton, England, and one of a large family. He was educated by his father, who was master of the grammar school, and who wanted him to study to be a doctor. At last his father allowed him to have his way in studying to become an artist, so eager he was about it. He went up to London at about the age of seventeen and for two years devoted himself to acquiring a knowledge of this art under the painter Thomas Hudson, with whom he was very happy. Then back again to his own home he journeyed and painted portraits of the folk in the little town where he lived.

Then, upon the invitation of one of his friends, who was a soldier and sailor and in command of a warship, he sailed to Italy. He stayed in Rome for several years, studied the marvelous works of the great Michelangelo and Raphael—declaring that Michelangelo was the greatest of all artists. In Rome, where there were such wonderful art treasures, he was very happy, though he grew homesick for England, his family and friends.

So he returned to London and opened a studio where he began portrait painting as a profession, and was kept very busy, for many wanted him to paint their portraits. Aided by the careful education given him by his father as well as his own pleasing personality and charming manners, he soon made friends among the great and noble of the day and acquired a brilliant reputation that brought him more orders than he could fill and made necessary the employment of assistants. He soon moved to a more beautiful home, where he placed the pictures he owned, and lived with his sister who kept house for him and took care of him.

With all these honors and activities—for at the height of his success he painted one hundred and fifty portraits a year—he found time to travel to Belgium and Holland and study the masterpieces of these countries in order to take home suggestions from the famous painters of old and thereby improve his own work.

He numbered among his subjects the most famous men of the age—Dr. Johnson, Edward Gibbon, Oliver Goldsmith and members of the nobility as well. The most beautiful women in England were among those who sat for him. His portraits were simple and revealed the character of each person.

Joshua Reynolds knew just how to paint boys and girls, perhaps better than he did grown folk. He won their confidence, made them his friends, and so caught just the expressions he wished. Who has not enjoyed the little Strawberry Girl with her demure smile and big eyes, Miss Bowles so natural and happy, small Georgiana Augusta Frederica Seymour, the delightful small girl in "The Age of Innocence"? They are all so simple and happy and childlike, each one looking for all the world as if she and the artist were having a very good time together. Sometimes he made them act parts, one of his pictures being of a little English boy dressed as King Henry the Eighth and looking very important indeed!

Joshua Reynolds helped found a school, the Royal Academy, where young artists were taught to draw and to paint, and where pictures were exhibited each year, and he was made president of it. That was surely a great honor and he received another very great one—he was knighted by his king, King George the Third, for the wonderful pictures he painted. Thus he became Sir Joshua!

Some Paintings by Sir Joshua Reynolds:

THE AGE OF INNOCENCE
National Gallery, London
PORTRAIT OF MASTER JOHN CREWE IN THE CHARACTER OF HENRY THE EIGHTH
Collection of the Earl of Crewe, Crewe, England
ANGELS' HEADS (*Series of Portraits of Little Frances Gordon*)
National Gallery, London
LITTLE MISS BOWLES
Wallace Collection, London
LADY CAROLINE HOWARD
National Gallery of Art, Washington
SARAH SIDDONS AS THE TRAGIC MUSE
Henry E. Huntington Art Gallery, San Marino, California
JANE, COUNTESS OF HARRINGTON
Henry E. Huntington Art Gallery, San Marino, California
PORTRAIT OF MISS BARNARD
Berkshire Museum, Pittsfield

Thomas Gainsborough lived at the same time as Joshua Reynolds. His father was a merchant of Sudbury who, convinced that his son had artistic gifts, sent him to London to study painting. So successful were his portraits that he became a painter of Royalty. There was a natural rivalry between Reynolds and Gainsborough and the latter seemed to repel the friendly advances of Reynolds, causing a coolness that ceased only in his last illness, when he sent for Sir Joshua to thank him for the good opinion he had held of him. Each portrait painter had a very high opinion of the other. Gainsborough died in 1788, four years earlier than Reynolds.

In his paintings Gainsborough used only soft, cool colors, dull reds and pinks, silver grays and blues. His famous "Blue Boy," as you will learn from the story, was painted to prove that Sir Joshua was wrong when he said that the masses of light in a picture should always be warm and mellow and that cool colors should be used only as a background and contrast to set off the more vivid hues. Gainsborough therefore painted the boy in cool blue to illustrate his idea, but he broke the blue with the mellow brown background.

Some of Gainsborough's Pictures:

PORTRAIT OF MRS. SIDDONS
National Gallery, London

PORTRAIT OF LITTLE MISS HAVERFIELD
Wallace Collection, London

THE WATERING PLACE
National Gallery, London

A CHILD WITH A CAT
Metropolitan Museum of Art, New York

ENGLISH LANDSCAPE
Metropolitan Museum of Art, New York

MRS. RICHARD BRINSLEY SHERIDAN
National Gallery of Art, Washington

THE ARTIST'S DAUGHTERS, MARGARET AND MARY
Art Museum, Worcester

THE COTTAGE DOOR
Henry E. Huntington Art Gallery, San Marino, California

THE HONORABLE FRANCES DUNCOMBE
Frick Collection, New York
EDWARD AND WILLIAM TOMKINSON
Taft Museum, Cincinnati

TWO PAINTERS WHO LOVED CHILDREN

Two boys, with only three years' difference between them, were attending school at the same time in England more than two hundred years ago—one in the Sudbury Grammar School in Suffolk, the other in the Plympton Public School in Devonshire.

Both liked to draw better than to do anything else! Both grew up to be great artists, recognized by king and nobles, enjoyed by the people of their day and of all the years which have gone winging by since then.

Thomas Gainsborough was the youngest of five boys in the Gainsborough family at Sudbury. Besides, he had four sisters, all older than himself. Tom sometimes could persuade one or another of them to do his school exercises so that he might have time to draw!

"Be careful," his sisters, however, would warn him. "Uncle Burroughs will find you out yet!" Sometimes it was an advantage to have an uncle for a schoolmaster. Sometimes it was not! As, for instance, when a fellow wanted to get excused for a day and go off by himself where he could see the velvety green fields and the cows blinking at him; the apple trees blossoming all pink and white, the river like a silvery blue stream framed in green. Those were to Tom more important than grammar or sums, pictures he just had to paint! And he must find a way to make Uncle Burroughs let him go. Why, he was so very hardhearted that he had refused his request many a time!

"If you please, sir," bowed Tom again in his very best manner one morning, a gorgeous morning with every beauty of color and pattern of light and of shadow brought out in grass, in trees, in flowers and in sky. How the glorious sun did shine! Tom looked pityingly at his classmates, cooped up in the schoolroom, as the master slowly read the words upon the paper Tom had handed him:

"Give Tom a holiday," signed with a flourishing "J.G."

"Humph!" muttered his uncle. "I shall have to speak to John about giving in so readily to Tom's whims. The lad needs his schooling." Then, aloud, "Since your father has requested it, I will let you go this time. But remember, never again. What do you need of holidays? You, whose wits are always taking a holiday from the sums I set you?"

Tom waited to hear no more but bounded quickly away —before Uncle Burroughs should change his mind. He knew his father was likely to discover that he had imitated his writing, but he had a whole day before him in which he could draw whatever came to his fancy.

He penciled pictures of delicate flowers, of bent old trees casting their patterns of shadows on the orchard grass. Sometimes he lay upon his back in the sweet grass and tried to picture the clouds. Towards sunset, after a day in which he had sketched to his heart's content, he stole towards home, a little apprehensive as to whether Uncle Burroughs had already found out about that forged note! He concealed himself among some bushes in his father's garden, and peeped out every now and then to see whether everything was still peaceful, or whether a storm had broken! Then his fancy was caught by a strangely shaped old tree, and he busied himself with making a sketch of it.

Just as he peered out for the dozenth time to make sure that all was well, the face of a man appeared at the top of the wall enclosing the garden, upturned as he gazed wistfully over the wall at a cluster of sun-ripened pears.

Tom caught the look of longing in his face as the slanting rays of the afternoon sun shone full upon it. Deftly his ever-ready pencil sketched him, delighting in the strong play of light and of shadow over his features. The man's hand reached up; cautiously he looked around, then he plucked one of the big, luscious pears, another and another, until he had his pockets full! Tom's pencil moved more and more swiftly. "If I can make it look like him, then Father can do something about catching this man who has been robbing us of our best pears! Then, perhaps Father will think that my picture making is worth while!"

But before he could show his father the portrait of the man who had been stealing his pears, he heard the stern command, "Thomas, I have seen the schoolmaster and the note you gave him. Such lack of sense of honor as you have shown will surely get you into serious trouble as well as bring disgrace upon your mother and me. If you keep on, one day you will be hanged!"

Tom hung his head. He did not want to hurt his parents, especially his mother, who had always shown him so much sympathy in his longing to make pictures. "But, Father," he began, taking a few halting steps forward, his sketch book in his hand, "let me show you—"

"Nay, you shall be severely punished for this act of disobedience and dishonesty. I am going to—"

"Wait a moment, John," begged Tom's mother, who had caught a glimpse of some of the sketches he had made during the day. "Give the boy a chance to show us what he has been up to in the time he has taken from school."

Tom showed them the old, gnarled tree he had sketched; it was so true they knew just where it stood in the orchard. The big, moss-covered rock, the wandering stream, the bushes topping the stone wall. The portrait of the man poking his head over the wall and reaching up his hand to take one of the golden pears. "Who is this?" his father exclaimed in amazement.

"Just a little while ago, when I was sketching that tree," answered Tom, gesturing excitedly, "the sun shone right on the face of this man who was stealing your pears! It was so easy to sketch him quickly with the lights and the shadows! It looks just like him, Father!"

" 'Tis the very scapegrace who has been hanging around the neighborhood! His living likeness, I'll be bound! The thief cannot deny his guilt when he sees this. Tom, I'm not going to punish you more than I have by telling you that your act of dishonesty today is a step towards becoming a dishonest person like this thief. Never take a holiday again through forging another's name. Keep on with your drawings at the proper times, not in school hours, and we shall be proud of you." He murmured to Tom's mother, proudly, as the boy walked away very much relieved, "Our Tom will be a genius and bring us great honor. Now to the catching of that pear-tree thief!"

Even as Tom Gainsborough's love of drawing sometimes led him astray, so did Joshua Reynolds'. He, too, much preferred to draw pictures than to study the Latin grammar set before him. Instead of having an uncle for a schoolmaster, Joshua had his own father! Day after day Latin exercises would be handed in with more attention to the drawings made on the back of them than to the construction of the sentences. His father slowly shook his head and sighed. Spoken words seemed to do no good, so under the drawing he wrote, "This is drawn by Joshua in school out of pure idleness."

"But, Father, I shall not need the Latin so much if I become an artist," Joshua would argue. "I would rather be an apothecary than any ordinary painter, but most of all I long to become a great painter."

Joshua was never idle in drawing, and his family was plenty large enough to give him all the practice he needed in making portraits. His sisters liked to draw, too, and at first did better than he. If paper and pencils were lacking, there were long stretches of whitewashed walls and burnt sticks!

It was just as hard to keep his mind on the sermon and his fingers quiet in church, as it was to keep his mind on his lessons and his fingers on the exercises and problems the master set him in school.

One Sunday, close on to his twelfth birthday, he sat up very straight by the side of one of his chums in a little church, not far from Plympton, and close to a Devonshire beach. The minister was a round-faced jolly-looking man, who also acted as a tutor to Dick Edgcumbe, the boy by Joshua's side.

His voice droned on. It was hot in the little church. Through the windows they could catch a glimpse of the waving grass and the sparkling sea. Joshua stifled a yawn just as Dick nudged him, and without turning his head, whispered, "See if you can make a likeness of his round face! It is such a funny one, it will be fun to do it!"

Joshua let his eyes roam around him hunting for paper. Not a scrap in sight and he dared not use a hymnal. But he had a good broad thumb nail on his left hand, and Dick's pocket had yielded a pencil.

"Hurry!" whispered Joshua, when the last note of the last hymn was dying away. "Come on down to the beach to the boathouse. There are some ship's paints nearby and I can copy his moon face before I forget it!"

Down to the shore dashed the boys, nimbly dodging all who would have words with them. Sure enough! Not only were there paints and a brush in the old boathouse, but a canvas—part of an old sail.

"It is like him!" praised Dick enthusiastically. "Won't he scowl when he sees it!"

"My first oil painting," chuckled Joshua. "Only I wouldn't choose ship's paints and an old piece of sail! I must have good tools to become a great painter!"

Both Joshua and Tom fulfilled their ambition to become artists. Both boys brought honor to their families. In their day they were acclaimed in London and throughout England. Today they are renowned all over the whole world.

Thomas Gainsborough never ceased to love all the beauties of the countryside, the velvety fields, the bent old trees, the deep, still woods, the shining rivers. "Ah! there is an apple tree like the one close by our door at home!" someone in London would say. "The very lane, or at least its double, down which I used to walk each day after the farm work was done!" another would remember. "He brings back to us all the beauty of the color and fragrance of the countryside! He is our finest landscape artist."

He became, too, one of England's greatest portrait painters, like that other boy, Joshua Reynolds. Not only did he make true likenesses, bringing out the beauty and charm of the court ladies, the simplicity and naturalness of his daughters and the other children he painted, but he placed each figure in a most happy setting, whether it be of a stately garden or of very natural country trees. Always he brought forth all the beauty of color in the harmony he planned. "His hand is as light as the sweep of a cloud, as swift as the flash of a sunbeam," Mr. Ruskin praised him.

Many great men and women sat for Thomas Gainsborough and Joshua Reynolds to have their portraits painted, and so have become more real and more human to us. Even the King, the same King George who did so much to hasten the Declaration of Independence of the colonies in America, summoned him to court. "This artist shall paint his King and his Queen," he commanded. After that, of course, Thomas Gainsborough received many orders from courtiers and ladies, for to have one's portrait painted by Gainsborough was all the fashion!

As for Joshua Reynolds, the same King George knighted him, the artist of England who had been made president of the Royal Academy, the school where pupils were taught and pictures exhibited each year. It was a very great honor to be elected president of that school, and a greater honor to be knighted by his King because of his beautiful pictures. Just as when a brave man of long ago, because of his deed of valor, knelt before his King and received the accolade of knighthood, and heard the words, "Rise, Sir Knight!" so did Joshua Reynolds become Sir Joshua because of his wonderful pictures. Although he painted many great and famous people, he liked best of all to make pictures of children. He knew just what to say to them to get the very expressions he wanted. And it is because of these pictures of boys and girls that we know him best.

You all know little Miss Bowles! In order to get acquainted with her and win her liking, the artist sat by her side at a dinner to which he was invited at her house. Such wonderful stories he told! Such magical tricks he played!

"Just look over there at that picture on the opposite wall!" he persuaded her. When she looked back again, her plate had disappeared! And somehow or other it came back again without her knowing it. No wonder she was glad to go to his house the next day and watch him manage his long-handled brushes as she sat before him, very naturally playing with her favorite dog, and listening to his stories. For was he not the best playfellow in the world? And no wonder that Sir Joshua caught on her little face the very expression he wanted!

Sir Joshua had said in one of his discourses, delivered before the students of the Royal Academy, "It ought, in my opinion, to be indispensably observed that the masses of light in a picture be always of a warm, mellow colour, yellow, red, or a yellowish-white and that the blue, the grey, or the green colours be kept almost entirely out of these masses, and used only to support and set off these warm colours; and for this purpose, a small proportion of cold colours will be sufficient."

"Not at all," disagreed Thomas Gainsborough, who shared with Sir Joshua the honors of successful portraiture. "A most beautiful picture can be painted in which the principal color is blue!"

"It will be too cold for beauty," asserted his rival quite as firmly.

"You shall soon see," promised Mr. Gainsborough. "Already my picture has taken shape and color.

"Humph!" he muttered to himself, as day after day after day he worked in his London studio, so delighted with the grace of the boy whose portrait he was painting, and the solution of the problem before him, that the hours fairly flew. "I will show Sir Joshua and those of his opinions a thing or two!" Whereupon he flourished his long-handled brushes, stepped back from the boy so easily and naturally posed before him, looked at him keenly, and went back to his painting with renewed delight.

Spellbound stood the people before that picture when it was exhibited.

"So simple in arrangement," murmured some, as they gazed at the boy in his costume of blue silk with rich lace at the neck and wrists, embroidery at the edge of his short-waisted jacket, his white silk stockings held by lace-trimmed garters, a large hat adorned with a soft white feather, in his hand.

"Such a fine looking boy. I know who he is—Master Buttall. And so like a real boy, nothing forced about the way he is standing but so natural, and direct in treatment."

"Mr. Gainsborough has won his contention," one and another agreed. "A harmony of cool colors, blues and green-blues almost like the deep colors in some of the Chinese vases. Though the colors are cool, yet they seem soft and mellow. Perhaps the warm tones in the landscape behind the boy, in the trees and the sky, help break the effect of the blues. Were this the only picture he ever painted, 'twould make him famous!"

GILBERT STUART

1755–1828

BEFORE THE STORY

DID you ever think you'd like to become a portrait painter and do honor to men and women, help make them live in the years to come?

As we have seen, kings and queens like to have painters live at their courts so that they may have their likenesses put upon canvas; they know they will live in this way in the years to come. Court writers may tell all about their rulers in words, and people who have very good imaginations will construct good likenesses from the word pictures; but each might build up a picture in his mind just a little different from all the others! And most people want something to see. So, court painters are always very necessary to their rulers.

We should have lost a great deal had it not been for our portrait artists who have made live upon their canvases these great minds and hearts and souls who helped make our country what it is today. And Gilbert Stuart is one of the greatest of these. To him we owe the portraits of our first president, George Washington, which are famed throughout the world and known and revered by every man and woman and boy and girl in our country. A great writer, Mark Twain, once said: "If George Washington should rise from the dead, and should not resemble the Stuart portrait, he would be denounced as an impostor!"

Gilbert Stuart painted not only a likeness of the physical features of those who sat for him—he did not consider that was enough for a true portrait painter—but he brought out the inner person as well. He portrayed the great heart and mind which made up the character of George Washington. He made us feel acquainted with him.

Gilbert Stuart was born in 1755 at Narragansett, R. I., and began painting portraits when, as a boy of thirteen, he was presented with a box of paints and some brushes by a doctor friend of the family.

When he was about twenty, and well started in his profession of portrait painting, the Revolutionary War was imminent in America, and Gilbert Stuart, who belonged to a Tory family, went to London to seek his fortune. There he met and studied with Benjamin West and won fame as a portrait painter.

When he returned to America after the Revolution, and established a studio in Philadelphia, it was George Washington he wanted to paint. Many likenesses he painted of him and he also painted a portrait of John Quincy Adams. Always he was able to bring forth the true character of the person, as well as the physical likeness. He said, "I work to express sentiment, grace and character."

Gilbert Stuart died in 1828 in Boston, where he lived the last twenty years of his life.

Some of Gilbert Stuart's Portraits:

PORTRAIT OF BENJAMIN WEST
National Portrait Gallery, London

PORTRAIT OF MARTHA WASHINGTON (*unfinished*)
Museum of Fine Arts, Boston

PORTRAIT OF HIMSELF (*unfinished sketch*)
Metropolitan Museum of Art, New York
PORTRAIT OF JAMES MONROE
Metropolitan Museum of Art, New York
PORTRAIT OF JOSEF DE JAUDENS Y NEBOT
Metropolitan Museum of Art, New York
PORTRAIT OF MRS. RICHARD YATES
National Gallery of Art, Washington
PORTRAIT OF PETER STUYVESANT
Historical Society, New York

GILBERT STUART, THE PAINTER OF OUR FIRST PRESIDENT

Gilbert Stuart stood upon the deck of the last ship which left Boston harbor before the Revolutionary War. The day following, the Battle of Bunker Hill occurred, when well-trained British soldiers learned no longer to make light of the courage of the untrained rebel farmers. On that day all ships were detained within the harbor. So Gilbert Stuart left just in time.

" 'Twill be no place for an artist should war come," he thought to himself, as he watched the distance slowly grow between the sturdy little boat upon which he sailed and the mist-wrapt shore. "Had I stayed, no knowing when I might have visited London and Paris and Rome to study the art galleries there. With my staunch old father under His Majesty's flag in Nova Scotia, and myself on the way to England, the colonies are well rid of such Tory sympathizers—though 'tis not likely that they will break with our motherland. At any rate, I'll be sure to paint more portraits on the other side of the water than here."

With his father a staunch supporter of the crown, and brought up by him to revere England and England's King, it was not strange that the young painter failed to respond to the call of the patriots. He escaped to a place where he could study the art in which he longed to improve.

But London was such a big city and he had so little money. The American-born artist, Benjamin West, now high in the favor of His Majesty, was the one he must see, he decided, as soon as he got his "land legs" back after three months in a little vessel upon a most restless and uncertain sea. Yet months went piling up into one year and well into another before he went to see him, although Benjamin West was well known to be a friend to all young artists whom he could help in any way.

As a boy he had made his brushes from the fur of his father's pet cat, colors from the juice of berries, indigo from his mother's washtub, and the colors the Indians gave him.

One evening he was dining, as was his custom, with some of the guests who could always be found at his London home.

"If you please, sir," apologized one of his servants, "a young man is calling to see you."

"Can he not come at some other time of the day or night than when I am entertaining and being more delightfully entertained by my friends? Who is he?"

"If you please, sir, I do not know but he says he came from America."

"Ah!" beamed the kind old painter, "bring the lad in! Gentlemen, any young artist from that land where I had my first dreams and struggles and help is indeed welcome. We must see what we can do to aid him."

A tall young man in a fashionably cut green coat awaited the older artist from America, who had won fame even from the King of England and his court.

"I have long desired to see you, sir," he said, bowing before the older painter, of whom he had so often heard, "for I want to make progress as a portrait painter." Benjamin West looked at some of his pictures and promptly offered to take him as a student.

"You shall live here in my home," offered the kind old artist from Philadelphia, "and it may be that you can help me as much as I help you. I think that I see one way of your aiding me, for you bear a striking likeness to King Charles the First of England and I shall put the robes of the Garter upon you when I paint the portrait of him for his present Majesty!"

"This portrait must be finished on the morrow," declared His Majesty's painter, Benjamin West, rather anxiously one day, "and I have this big historical canvas to work up as well. Do you, Stuart, work upon the portrait and have it ready in the early morning, mind you." Well did the master know that his young pupil could surpass him in the matter of portraits!

True to his promise the portrait was finished early the next morning; but when the master entered the room, immaculate, hair powdered, white silk stockings without a wrinkle, yellow morocco slippers, a fencing bout was at its height between his pupil, Gilbert Stuart, and his son, Rafe! They were making so much noise that they did not know they were being sternly and reprovingly observed.

"There, you dog!" cried Stuart, lunging with his maulstick in mock earnestness upon his master's son, standing against one of his father's pictures; "I have you, and nothing but your background relieves you!"

Looking up they saw Benjamin West frowning, yet with a smile threatening to soften the stern lines.

"Mr. Stuart," he said very sternly, "is this the way you treat me and betray my trust in you?"

"Why, sir," answered his pupil in rather an aggrieved tone of voice, "no harm is done! We were only in fun, and I have hurt neither your son nor the background of your picture against which he is standing!"

"What about my portrait I asked you to finish?" sternly reminded the old artist. "It was promised for this morning and now you have betrayed my trust in you. You have broken your promise and indulged in this foolish prank. How can you hope to become a true painter of portraits if you neglect the rare chances I give you? Have you no greater sense of honor, no more devotion to your work? Answer me, sir!"

"Do not condemn me, sir," begged his pupil, "before you look at the portrait. It is finished and I hope that it has your approval."

Surprised, the master carefully examined it. "Forget what I have said," he made amends warmly. "It is well done. I was sure I could trust you, and I am equally sure that as a painter of portraits you will hold your own on both sides of the Atlantic. You are ready to open a studio of your own!"

"Six sitters a day," Stuart decided upon. "They are enough. Then down go my palette and brushes and out I rush to enjoy a walk in the park. Then home and dinner and songs and stories with good friends—my old master, the King's painter, Sir Joshua Reynolds, Mr. Gainsborough—and musicians and actors as well as painters. Good fellows, all!"

Dukes and admirals and lords and even kings and

princes sat to him for their portraits and his reputation as a fine portrait painter grew. "I have been away from America long enough!" he at last declared. "After all, home is on the other side of the ocean, where there is a great and noble man whom it is my ambition to paint if it is the last portrait I put upon canvas. That man is George Washington! Although my money is low, as it always is from what my old master calls my extravagant way of living, yet I am sure that I can get passage by painting a portrait of the ship's owner!"

"He belongs to us!" cried his countrymen welcoming him as he landed in New York. "He has won fame and honor across the waters in the land from which we won our independence, but this is his native land and we need him here to make our leaders live forever! Welcome to Gilbert Stuart, our painter of America!"

"Let me paint the likeness of the leader of America!" ventured the artist, telling of the ambition and hope which was strong in his heart. "Then shall I be doing America a great service. I promise you his true likeness, the expression of his eyes, the strength of his mouth, a glimpse of his soul; and in colors so lifelike, so natural, that you shall protest he is in flesh and blood before you. I am here to serve you as I can."

When Congress was in session in Philadelphia Gilbert Stuart went there, happy because of a letter of introduction to the President of the United States of America, whom he so much admired. And the portrait painter who had talked freely with great men in Europe, chatting and laughing that he might bring to their faces the expression he wished to capture upon his canvas, found himself almost tongue-tied in the presence of the man of America he so longed to paint.

Dressed in black velvet, with white lace ruffles and

cravat, George Washington sat quietly before his portrait painter—simple, patient, serene, dignified, a leader in war and in peace.

"I put myself into your hands, sir, at the request of my wife and the people of America, though I shall not at first be a patient sitter. No doubt in time I shall be able to take and hold any pose you may wish with a fair amount of eagerness and interest."

"I shall not paint you as the General of the armies who won independence, sir; I knew you not then. I shall paint you in the time of peace as President of the United States. So, I think, will the people wish to remember you."

Then, looking earnestly at the man posed before him, the artist took his position, standing before his easel, his hand trembling with an unsteadiness he always had to combat. A long look he gave the man before him and a searching look as if he would read his very soul and draw it to the surface. Then, when his hand became more steady, quickly, with short, decided, and sure touches of the brush he laid his colors upon the canvas, making the flesh seem to glow and throb with life.

"Nay, sir, it is no concern of mine what costume you wear, whether lace at the wrists or a ruffle at the throat. 'Tis the face I am after, the mellow glow of the flesh, the light and the shadow, the character behind that lights it with expression. Clothes belong to tailors who make them their business; I copy the works of God! The grace, the character, the feeling of the man I work to imprison upon my canvas. You, sir, shall live not only in the minds and the hearts of your fellow citizens but in their eyes as well, if my brushes will but obey their master." That they did obey, the whole world knows!

One of the portraits of George Washington was placed in the White House, the home of our Presidents, and admired by all visitors. When James Madison became President he had the sweet and kind Dolly Madison as wife to help him not only in the festivities but in the national affairs as well. Her tact and good judgment helped him decide wisely many an important national question and were ready to meet any crisis.

Once again war was declared—a second time with England—and one August day the British troops marched against the capital.

"Alas, alas!" mourned everyone. "Fifty British ships are anchoring in the Potomac. We have no time to lose but must flee with all our valuables, for our homes will surely be destroyed! And no doubt our lives are threatened as well."

"Save the state papers and documents!" cried President Madison as he rode away to where the citizens of Washington were gathering as soldiers to plan what they could do to save their city. After some hours a note from him was given to the brave Dolly Madison, who was willing to stay in the White House and meet whatever came. "The enemy is strong and may destroy the city. Be ready to leave at a moment's warning."

At once the brave mistress of the White House began to pack the nation's treasured papers. As she worked she could hear the cannon. How she longed for her husband to return! But the President of the United States, like his brave wife, was serving his country before himself.

A long night passed and she waited alone, with only a few servants and friends to protect her and with a battle raging near. Morning brought no message. In midafternoon two dust-covered horsemen galloped to the White House. "Fly!" they cried. "Lose not a moment! The enemy is advancing! Fly for your lives!"

Hastily a wagon was loaded with the White House

silver and valuable papers. "Hasten!" begged the frightened group who aided her. "The British will soon be here and 'tis said the British Admiral and his officers have boasted that they will make you and President Madison prisoners!"

Grimly the President's wife finished her task. She was just about to be driven hurriedly away when she remembered. "Wait! I must save the portrait of our first President! Gilbert Stuart's likeness of Washington shall never fall into British hands!"

Bordered by a heavy frame the famous portrait of the man who had proved himself to be first in the hearts of his countrymen, had been screwed into its place on the wall.

"Hurry! Hurry!" the frantic servants and friends cried.

"Take the canvas from the frame," commanded Dolly Madison as the roar of the enemy's guns grew louder, "and roll it carefully. The Declaration of Independence is still in its case apart from the other papers. I must save that, too."

No sooner had they driven rapidly away, than the British troops appeared and broke into the White House; soon it was in flames. But Dolly Madison had saved the portrait to which Gilbert Stuart had summoned the very spirit of George Washington.

JEAN BAPTISTE COROT

1796–1875

BEFORE THE STORY

Jean Baptiste Camille Corot called his friend Rousseau an "Eagle" among painters, and himself "but a fluttering lark." When we look at Corot's pictures, happy in subject and soft in blue and silver colors, we understand why that name remained with him and why he was often called the "Skylark of Painters." Springtime was the season he liked, when the trees blossom in soft gray-green and the birds sing their welcoming songs. That is the time of year Corot especially pictured. Like the good Saint Francis of Assisi who loved the birds so well that they gathered around him and sang to him, so did Jean Baptiste Corot understand them and in some of his early morning pictures we can almost hear the birds singing their welcome to the light and warmth of the new day.

Corot tells in his picture-songs with his language of Line and Light and Shadow and especially Color, soft blue and silvery-gray, of his love for smiling Mother Nature. Unlike his friend Rousseau, who often pictured the more rugged side of Nature, or Diaz, who sometimes captured the majesty of a stormy sky, Corot loved the serene blue sky, cloudless save for a thin silver-blue haze like a delicate veil which lessens the glow of the sun. He tells of the yielding earth from which tender grass and opening buds peer forth. Corot thought Springtime was the loveliest time of all the year and his poem-pictures of it make us agree with him.

1796, not long after the close of our Revolutionary War, is the year in which he was born in Paris, still a turbulent year in France, though the French Revolution was drawing to a close. His father was something between a hairdresser and a merchant, his mother a designer of hats. Both were important personages, and his mother was always so busy making elegant hats for fashionable ladies that sometimes she did not have time to take care of her babies. Camille and his sister were sent for four years to a little village where a foster mother cared for them.

When Camille was eleven years old he went to school in Rouen, and there he met a friend who, like him, loved Nature, and the two of them took long walks out into the countryside, spending the whole day there. Then he was happy, for the trees, the birds, the flowers, the green grass, and the blue sky were his friends.

At sixteen years of age he had finished his school studies and tried his luck as a clerk with a dealer in fancy goods and with a cloth merchant. But he did not fit into that life for his mind was intent upon picturemaking, which did not make him very valuable to those who would teach him a trade! Picturemaking was the one thing he wanted to do, the one thing which made him happy.

The river Seine with its ships and tree-lined banks afforded him material for many sketches, but Ville d'Avray, four miles from Paris, where his father bought a little house, was his especial delight. Plenty of leafy branches, grasses, birds, a pond or lake or river—and the blue sky overhead, were all that he asked for. With these to imitate in color he was completely happy. Many pictures suggested themselves in the changing lights of day—the gathering mists rising over the lake, the wind blowing up soft, fluffy clouds in the sky.

Bordering the old Forest of Fontainebleau is the little

village of Barbizon where, in the time of Corot, painters went that they might picture the beauties of Nature as they actually saw them, morning, noon and night, before and after a storm, the dew sparkling on the leafy branches. Many of the pictures painted in that Forest by the Barbizon painters—Corot, Millet, Rousseau, Daubigny, Diaz, and the others upon whose canvases the beauties of Nature were most truly reflected—today bring fortunes, whereas in the days of the painters they sometimes did not bring enough to pay the bills of everyday living! Corot's pictures brought so little that his parents helped him with an allowance for his daily living until he was over fifty.

A trip to Italy! How Camille Corot did enjoy it, and how eagerly he studied there, introducing into his pictures the Cathedral dome of Florence and its surrounding hills, a glimpse of the historic Roman Forum.

Nor was Corot without recognition or reward to encourage him. When two medals for the excellence of his pictures were awarded him, his family and his friends realized that he had chosen the profession best for him after all; especially when he received his Cross of the Legion of Honor.

Some pictures are more like beautiful prose and some more like poetry. Corot's are like the latter, with simple verses of beautiful design and delicate color rhythms. Whereas Rousseau and the other painters, who went to live near the Forest of Barbizon that they might copy the moods of Nature, were more or less exact in their interpretations, the poet, Corot, gave play to his fancy, adding his imagination and dreams to what he saw in Nature. Camille Corot was happy with his picture-poems, his love of instrumental and vocal music, his devotion to his family, and his ability to make them happy.

The painter of the "Angelus" and "The Gleaners," Jean François Millet, was a great friend of Corot's. When, after Millet's death, Corot received a fairly large sum of money from a picture dealer, he directed that it be sent to the widow of his friend, Millet. "But," he said, "she must believe that you have bought pictures from him." That little episode will speak eloquently of his kindness and generosity. "Father Corot" people called him, for he was a great favorite among all who knew him.

Some of Corot's Pictures:

Dance of the Nymphs
Louvre, Paris
Morning
Louvre, Paris
Ville d'Avray
Metropolitan Museum of Art, New York
Ville d'Avray: Wooded Banks of the Pool with a Woman Gathering Fagots
Metropolitan Museum of Art, New York
River Scene
Metropolitan Museum of Art, New York
A View near Volterra
National Gallery of Art, Washington
Agostina
National Gallery of Art, Washington
Bacchante by the Sea
Metropolitan Museum of Art, New York
Landscape
Museum of Fine Arts, Springfield
Montigny les Cormeilles
Farnsworth Museum of Wellesley College

JEAN BAPTISTE COROT: A PAINTER OF SPRINGTIME

"Whatever are we going to do with our son Camille?" scolded Marie Corot, as she sat in her shop in Paris, her fingers busy with a hat which she had designed for a very grand lady, while the boy's father, Louis Jacques, bent over the books which held the accounts. "We have had him taught under good teachers in college at Rouen and at Poissy. We have found him a place as salesman in three of the best drapery houses—but no! He cares only for the making of pictures!"

The boy's father sighed. "Camille always was a strange lad, wanting a pencil or a bit of charcoal in his hand, always watching the sky, the clouds, and the tree tops, and laughing aloud at sunshine and colors—that strange young one! See, here are his sketches all over these books and the counter of the shop. He can no more keep from picturemaking than you can from hat blocking and hat trimming; or I from combing and curling hair to make a becoming crown to the face! So you see, Marie," and his eyes twinkled as he briskly crossed the room to lay his hand for a moment upon her shoulder, "it is really not strange, for we could not take pleasure in selling goods any more than he can. Come, disappointed though we may be, let the lad have his way; and we will give him enough to feed him and house him and buy his clothes and his brushes. It may be that a year of this foolish business will cure him and then we can afford to set him up in some trade which will bring him a good return.

"Ah there, Camille, I was about to send for you! Since you will never become a cloth merchant but are determined to spend all your time in the painting of pictures, go on amusing yourself in this way, and we will help you. But mind, we don't approve!"

"Victoire! Victoire!" Camille called to his sister, "at last I am free to do what I love with all my heart! I shall be a painter with our parents' consent, and will straightway enter some studio to learn before I set up for myself. Victoire, I never was so happy! Just wait until I get to the Ville d'Avray where the trees and the grasses sway in the breeze, and the flowers nod, and a silver-blue mist rises from the pond, and the birds sing. Then I shall paint some real pictures! Already I see them in my mind and dream of them. I shall paint an early morning picture with the dew on the grass and the flowers, one in which the wind is bending the trees and making them dance, as it did the last time we were there.

"I shall paint the old boatman on the river, a path through the trees in the wood which meet overhead like an arch. Perhaps I shall paint the silvery moon journeying across the sky. I've always fancied the moon a shepherdess and the fleecy white clouds her sheep! Often the wind drives the clouds far apart, and I wonder how the shepherdess can ever get her flock together again."

"Camille, your pictures shall sing with the beauties of Nature, so that all folk will like them!"

"Did I not tell you, Victoire?" exulted the delighted painter as he and his sister wandered among the trees near the little country house in the Ville d'Avray. "Here I have everything which goes to the making of pictures—whereas in the studio there are only copies of Nature and I am stifled by the many buildings which shut out the sky. I've studied it all in the sunlight and bathed in the moonbeams which give a very different effect, I assure you, Victoire. Will you not walk with me tonight beneath these featheryfoliaged branches, close to the moon-drenched pond? See, the little new moon is just appearing! And it is all so still! Nothing can be heard but the wind in the trees, whispering its secrets!"

"A walk in the moonlight suits me well enough, Camille," laughed his younger sister, Victoire; "but a walk at dawn such as you often take would please me not at all. I am a sleepyhead and have not the urge of art to awake me! Let Rose share your morning walks."

"You can't tease me, Victoire. Rose is one of the finest girls in my mother's shop and has a true love of beauty. She shall walk with me whenever she chooses, and talk with me whenever we both choose, and that's all there is to it! Here is a surprise for you. One of my pictures of this forest which I sent to the Exhibition at the Salon, has won me a medal! Now perhaps our father and mother will take my work seriously! 'Why,' my father will say, 'I do believe Camille has real talent after all!' "

"We all know it now," answered Victoire, her eyes shining. "The good Father whose little church stands yonder says that he is going to ask you to paint religious stories upon its walls."

Italy was a very wonderful land and Corot learned a great deal from the Masters there, but he was glad to get home again and out among the trees by his favorite pond. Sometimes he was up as early as three o'clock in the morning to get the effects he wanted, singing at the top of his voice as he worked, for there was no fear of disturbing his neighbors there.

"I sing because I feel as happy as the birds out here so close to the earth and the sky, the birds and the flowers. All my life my needs will be an easel and palette, a hat to protect me from the sun at noonday, my long blue blouse to make me one with the color harmony around me, and perhaps a bit of bread to eat if I think of it, and my pipe at hand. The beauties of Nature around me are enough to satisfy the wants of any man! Brush in hand, I listen to the birds' songs, the rustling of the wind among the leaves, the music of the rippling waves upon the shore. I see the clouds gather, the blue mist arise, the shadows reflected in the quiet water. I am alone with Nature and her beauty, and then I can paint what I see and feel.

"Nature 'resembles a white sheet' early in the morning, 'on which is scarcely visible the outlines of a few great masses of things. Everything is perfumed and all trembles under the freshening breezes of dawn. Bing! The sun gets clearer; but it has not yet torn away the veil of gauze behind which lie the meadow, the valley, the hills on the horizon. Bing! Bing! The first ray of the sun . . . another ray. Little flowers seem to awake joyously. Each has its trembling dewdrops. The quivering leaves are agitated by the breezes of the morning and in the trees invisible birds sing. It is as if the flowers offer up a prayer. The landscape lies entirely behind the transparent gauze of the ascending mist, gradually sucked up by the sun, which permits us to see, as it ascends, the silver-striped river, the meadows, the cottages, the far-receding distance. At last you can see what you imagined at first. Bam! The sun has risen. Bam! Everything sparkles, shines. Everything is full of light—light soft and caressing as yet. . . . The flowers lift up their heads. The birds fly here and there . . . and the artist paints away.' " *

"He is painting a poem," Rosa or some other friend would murmur, stealing away unobserved. "One can see the branches wave in the gentle breeze, feel the mist rise,

* *Said to be from Corot's letters to a friend. See Hoeber—Barbizon Painters.*

hear the birds sing, he is so in tune with Nature. Dear Father Corot! How everyone loves him!"

"The sun sinks towards the horizon. . . . It is time to get to work again . . . he throws his last ray, a streak of gold and purple fringing the flying cloud. . . . Twilight begins. . . . The sun is gone. . . . The meadows lose their colour . . . the trees are nothing but masses of brown and grey . . . the darkling waters reflect the soft tones of the sky. . . . Nature is drowsy. . . . All the same, the night breezes sigh among the leaves . . . birds, the voices of the flowers, say their prayers. . . . The nymphs are afoot . . . a star dives from the sky into the pond . . . whose shining is increased in the rippling of the water. . . . Good, my picture is made!" *

"It is beautiful," breathed Rosa and Victoire, "you make us see the picture you are going to paint. You bring out all the beauties of Nature."

"But I must stop now," gently murmured the painter. " 'My Heavenly Father has put out the lamp.' "

"Have you come to watch old Father Corot paint, my children?" gently asked Father Corot one sparkling spring day. "Sit here, Louis, and there, Paul, and hold Marie. And you must be very still—for see, there are birds perched upon the branches of the trees to watch me, too, and you must be as quiet as they are, for I want this picture to be good. I will tell you a secret which you must keep with me. 'There are days when it is I who paint; in those days the work is bad. The days when it is not I, an angel has come and worked for me; then it is good.' And this is one of those days! So be very quiet and watch carefully and you will see the buds burst forth into foliage, the trees grow, their branches move in the wind, and a mother and her little

* *From a letter said to have been written by Corot. See Everard Meynell's "Corot and His Friends," pp. 223, 224.*

daughter gather wood and walk down a path overarched by the great branches. If you are good you may join me in song."

"I will leave my picturemaking today," he decided one morning, carefully putting away his palette, his colors, and brushes. "It is a long time since I saw my good friend, Jean François Millet. Come, my beautiful Mother Marie, you need a change and the warm sunshine, so you shall ride with me to his vine-draped stone cottage."

Jean François Millet was busy working upon his picture of the "Man with the Hoe," which had called forth from his critics unpleasant remarks.

"Come, my good friend," smiled Corot, his eyes twinkling above his rosy cheeks and long, blue blouse. "It is time to rest for a while. Come with us for a ride down this tree-bordered road!"

"But my picture!" protested Millet. "It is not finished and time is pressing. What do you think of it, Friend Corot?"

"Your peasant pictures have depth and strength, but this one is so sober, Jean François. I like to picture the bright side of life. But you have painted long enough for today. Come out with me into the sunshine and the fragrance of the flower-laden air. It will do you good, and when you return you will be able to finish your peasant more quickly. Come, the change and the sunshine will surely make you more happy. Your pictures have greater depth than mine, but mine are happier. One day you will be painting those workers yonder, binding the grass into bundles, as the warm sunlight pours down."

"The pictures of Camille Corot are full of life," people declared. "There are those who draw better than he, but none who make their figures move more naturally, or belong more completely to the fields, the tree-shaded paths and the shores of the pond on which they stand. There is air in his pictures, and there are delicate mists which do away with hard outlines; a feeling of peace and quiet and fragrance. He deserves to be honored!"

"He is so good and kind," others added. "Never was there one more generous, always ready to help those less happy than he. Has he not given great gifts to our land during the siege of Paris by the Germans, that the suffering of those in distress may be relieved? Let us have a great celebration and honor him while he is with us to enjoy! Remember, he is seventy-eight years of age now."

At the Grand Hotel in Paris the celebration was held, with hundreds of people present, for all who knew him and his pictures loved him. A medal cast in gold was presented to him, and the old master, greatly pleased, said, "I am very happy to know that Father Corot is loved like this. I wish everyone might see and enjoy Nature as I do."

On another occasion when the Emperor, Napoleon the Third, decorated him with the Cross of the Legion of Honor, his old mother and father looked with awe on the tiny red ribbon which so many coveted and which their son was allowed to wear. The proud old father who had wanted his son to take up a trade, dazed but happy, told his neighbors, "Camille seemed foolish to us. He 'seems, after all, to have talent'!"

Camille Corot said of the medal, "I must hurry and paint good pictures, so that it cannot be said that I have stolen it. If only all people might enjoy Nature in all her beauty as I have been allowed to see it, all would be happier. I hope that when I have to leave this beautiful world I will be allowed to keep on with my pictures in the next." Just before he died, he said, "Last night I saw in a dream a landscape with a sky all rosy. It was charming and still stands before me quite distinctly; it will be marvelous to paint." Corot could say with the great poet, Robert Browning:

"The year's at the spring,
And day's at the morn;
Morning's at seven;
The hillside's dew pearled:
The lark's on the wing;
The snail's on the thorn;
God's in his heaven—
All's right with the world!"

JEAN FRANÇOIS MILLET

1814–1875

BEFORE THE STORY

JUST as anyone can best tell in words about what he really knows, what he has really seen and done, so can a painter best tell in pictures what he has really seen and lived. Some, it is true, like to tell about what they have heard, colored by their imaginations; some like to go far away from their homes into strange, colorful lands and picture the marvels to be found there. Some, like this artist, Jean François Millet, who lived in France a hundred years ago, are wise enough to tell about what they have really seen and known and felt in their own lives.

Millet was one of those who told in pictures the peasant life he had lived and seen all around him. He saw and pictured for all the simple beauty of the everyday life of the peasant folk. There was the daily toil in the fields; the moment of rest and prayer when the bells from the church tower sounded at evening; the sheep at the edge of the wood; a peasant woman spinning; the sower of seed in the fields; the first proud steps of a neighbor's baby; sunlight and shadow in the woods and the birds just bursting into song. All these simple, everyday scenes Millet painted so truthfully, so understandingly, and so beautifully that each, even the simplest, he made into a picture-poem.

Millet was born in 1814 in a humble peasant's cottage in the tiny French village of Gruchy, near Cherbourg. His father was a man of very fine character and his uncle was the village priest. Though he was brought up as a farm boy he had a good education and when he was twenty-three went to Paris to study and work. His years of faithful devotion to his art were rewarded, seven years before his death in 1875, by an award of the Legion of Honor by the French Government—a very great honor indeed.

Some of Millet's Works:

THE ANGELUS
Louvre, Paris
THE SHEPHERDESS
Louvre, Paris
AUTUMN
Metropolitan Museum of Art, New York
THE SOWER
Museum of Fine Arts, Boston
THE COOPER
Museum of Fine Arts, Boston
RETURN OF THE FLOCK
Pennsylvania Academy of the Fine Arts, Philadelphia
THE NEWBORN CALF
Art Institute, Chicago
DIGGERS (*etching*)
Wesleyan University Print Collection, Middletown, Connecticut

BEAUTY IN EVERYDAY WORK THROUGH THE EYES OF JEAN FRANÇOIS MILLET

The clear horizon stretched out to meet the vivid blue of the sea. Endlessly the waves beat against the high cliffs past which perhaps had sailed the ships of the Normans bent for conquest, many years before. But it was not the calling of the waves which Jean François Millet first remembered. Rather was it the soothing hum of the spinning wheel at which his grandmother worked in their thatched and vine-draped house, and her smile as she looked up from her work to see what he was doing. The sound of the wind could often be heard beating against the low, sturdy stone house perched so near to the edge of the cliff, almost like the nest of a bird, and almost as old as the bent elm tree close by. Another early memory was of his mother and father starting out for their work in the fields, and of him begging to go with them; the melody of the church bells ringing; the song of the birds.

"Up! Up, my small François!" sometimes his gentle grandmother would call him.

"Is it so late, Grandmother?" François would sleepily ask. "Have my mother and father gone to the fields? Is the jolly sun yet up?"

"Aye, wake up, my small François! Little do you know how long a time the birds have been singing the glory of God! And your mother and father at work in the fields these many hours."

"And I, who am named for the good Saint Francis of Assisi, who loved the birds, the trees and the flowers—my patron saint—still lie in bed!" said small François. Then wistfully, "I, too, love the birds, Grandmother. I love the way they fly so swiftly across the sky or sail over the fields of corn and grain. I love the beasties and the flowers, too. And sometimes when I draw the birds, they seem to speak to me as they did to the good Saint whose honored name I bear. Tell me again about them and him, please, Grandmother, before I go to find my mother and father in the fields."

"Full many a time, my François, hast thou heard the story of the good Saint Francis whose name crowns thee. Dost not remember how he made friends even with the wolf who had been frightening the folk of the village, eating their sheep and their cattle?"

François shuddered. He thought of his father's sheep, of his own pet lamb. He thought of the cows he had so often watched as they munched the sweet grass and turned to look at him with their great, dreamy eyes. He would not want any wolf to harm them!

"The good Saint Francis made the wolf feel sorry," his grandmother continued. "He told him that if he would promise not to harm the people or the animals of Assisi, the townsfolk would give him plenty of food to eat each day."

"And they shook hands on it—the wolf and Saint Francis, I remember! Now, Grandmother, Saint Francis and the birds!"

François had heard the story so many times, he could see it as a picture before him. Saint Francis in his long robe girded loosely at his waist, his sweet, friendly smile as he spoke to the birds fluttering and twittering around him, alighting upon his shoulders, upon his hands and feet, opening their beaks, spreading their wings, to show their delight in him.

" 'Birds, my brothers, you ought to praise your Creator

much, who clothed you in plumes, and gave you feathers for flying, who granted you the purity of the air, and without anxiety of yours directs you!' Thus did Saint Francis talk to his friends the birds, my François, and they answered him with their songs of praise. Did not the good Saint say that the birds, his brothers, sang more beautiful songs than he could to the praise of God? Did he not show his love by deeds as well as by words of praise—sharing his goods with the poor, doing good every day? That is the lesson for thee, his namesake, my François."

"That is what I would do, Grandmother," answered the boy, dreamily. "I, too, love the animals and the birds and would protect them and be kind to them. I, too, would do something to show my praise to the good God for this beautiful world in which we live, the great trees in the wood, the sparkling waves of the sea, the warm sun, the silver moon, and the twinkling stars. Most of all, Grandmother, more even than I love the sheep and the birds and the flowers, I love the people: those working in the fields, making hay, plowing, sowing, binding the sheaves; the mothers with their babies. I love them all, and when I grow up I mean to make pictures of them just as I have seen them. That is what I am going to do!"

His grandmother shook her head, and wondered as she watched him hurry off, a stocky little fellow in his worn homespun suit, his feet in their wooden shoes, whether his dreams would come true. He hurried to join the others at work in the fields, though well did she know that he drew pictures whenever he could get the chance! Did they not cover the floor, the walls, and even his wooden shoes? Many a time the neighbors had come to look at faithful pictures of themselves, or their children, their sheep, or their donkeys! Often there were hearty laughs at the rough pictures on the whitewashed walls, the neighbors good-naturedly laughing at themselves. Sometimes they looked with something like awe at the boy who worked in the fields with the rest of them, and yet who was so different from them all.

For work in the fields he must, as soon as he grew big enough. There were nine hungry mouths to be filled, and the stony soil was none too good to yield a harvest. So the work in the fields was hard, and all the boys and girls must help.

Jean Louis, his father, strong and gentle, loved by all his neighbors in the little hamlet, was an artist at heart. He led the village choir; he found beauty in the sunlight making golden the fields, in the patterns of light and of shadow in the great wood, nearby; in the flowers jeweled by the dew at the sun's rising. Work in the fields they must, and François, his eldest son, however much he liked to make pictures with charcoal, must work with them. How else could the fields be plowed, the seed sown, the harvest gathered? So work they did, in the summer time from dawn until sundown.

But Jean Louis understood his son, François, whose fingers were sensitive like his own, always finding their way to a bit of charcoal for the making of pictures, though he never complained of his share of the work in the fields. Sometimes, when they straightened their aching backs from raking the hay, or plowing the stubborn soil, and went to rest under the shade of a tree as they ate their simple lunch, Jean Louis would talk with his son of the beauties of Nature all around them.

"My son, lie down here in the grass, cooled by the shade of this bent old tree, and look up at the clear blue of the sky. See how it meets the deeper, wind-blown blue of the sea far out over the waters? What a picture it would make over yonder—our good neighbor's house peeping above the rise in the field. How tall this tree is, flowering from its trunk like a blossom from its stem. All around us the good God can be seen."

While his father and the other workers in the fields took their noonday sleep, François' fingers were busy. "I will picture this tree," he decided, "and surprise my father. I like the way the branches bend, and the patterns of the tender leaves. If I have time before they waken, I shall draw the house half hidden by the higher land. The one my father said would make such a good picture." His father lay very still, grateful for the rest and the shade. But he was not always asleep. Often, out of the corners of his eyes, he watched his son at his drawing, and planned for him just as he had earlier done for himself.

When the rainy days came and there could be no work in the fields, the boy pored over the old family Bible and studied and copied the engravings which pictured the stories. In the winter time, when François was not helping in the weaving of baskets, or listening, eager-eyed, to the old stories of his country, or following his father's lead in the singing of the old folk songs, he was busy making his pictures—everything that he saw around him, inside his home and without! The everyday, familiar things, and because of that very dear to him; the garden, the trees in the fields, the donkeys, the sheep, his grandmother or his sister at the spinning wheel. Familiar faces appeared on the floors, or the whitewashed walls. "Here am I! Here is Mother! Just look at Grandmother!" one and another would exclaim as they recognized the family portraits. "You have a son who is different from the rest of us," a neighbor would murmur, as he dropped in after a long day's work to look out towards the gold and crimson of the sunset across the water, and to talk about the harvest, or the news from Paris which had been brought by some wayfarer who was passing through their little village where he stopped to rest for an hour.

"Would that I could spare my son that he might become a painter of pictures!" François' father would sigh as he looked off towards the sunset, and wondered whether his dreams of picture making might not be one day fulfilled in his son.

It was a Sabbath day, and François had grown to be a young man. Still he worked hard in the fields with his parents and brothers and sisters. Still he enjoyed the sketches he made of the fields, the birds, the trees, the flowers, the people. His people they were, those by whose side he worked every day, whose sorrows and whose simple joys he shared.

They had all attended the little church which summoned them to rest and prayer. All the neighbors then walked slowly to their simple, thatched, stone homes. It was such a clear day that everything was strongly marked in outline. François left the others, and walked on ahead and alone. Suddenly he started. Along the road in front of him, clearly outlined in the sunlight, was an old man walking very slowly with dragging steps, pushing a wheelbarrow, his tall figure bent until his head seemed to be between his shoulders.

"Oh, for a piece of charcoal!" he thought to himself. "If only I might draw this bent figure here on this stone fence—just as I see it now, while it is yet before me!" Quickly, when he reached home, he took one of his precious pieces of charcoal and drew the old man while his bent form was still vivid in his memory.

"Aha! The bowed old man we passed today on the road!" exclaimed his brothers and sisters, returning from church. "How like him it is, even to his bent shoulders and his lagging steps!"

His father stood looking upon it for a long time. "My poor François," he said, "I see plainly that you are tormented by that idea of becoming an artist. I should have been very glad to send you to learn that painting business which they say is such a fine one, but I could not; you are the eldest of the boys and I needed you too much. Now your brothers are growing up and I will not keep you from learning what you wish so much to know. We shall journey to Cherbourg and find a painter there who will tell us whether you have the gift of making pictures, so that by doing so you can earn your daily bread."

"My father and the good God are kind," François confided to his grandmother. "If only the artist we visit shall see promise in my sketches!" And he worked hard on two more drawings to take with him. One was of a hillside with two shepherds and their sheep. The other was of a man giving bread to another hungry man under a starlit sky.

"Can it be true that I am really starting out to show my drawings to someone who will tell me what I can do?" sang François' heart. "Oh, how good it all is!" And he turned again to wave to his mother and his grandmother, who stood in the vine-framed doorway, and watched him and his father until they disappeared far down the road which led them towards the big towns and cities where real artists lived.

"Can it be that this boy has had no instruction?" the artist asked, amazed. "He has great promise! And thou," he turned to François' father, "thou wilt regret keeping him so long from his art, for he has in him the making of a great artist. Leave him here with me, and he shall draw what he likes and spend many hours before the great masters. One day I shall be proud that he has been my pupil, and you will be proud that he is your son!"

Many a time did François Millet think of those early days, after he had become a painter in Paris, where almost every day he went to the big Museum and learned from the great masters who had lived and gone, but who had left their work to inspire and help younger artists who were learning. "Such truth and strength and power in the great Michelangelo!" he murmured, standing longest before his mighty works. "Truly, such wonderful pictures of form! So shall mine be—true pictures of the folk I have seen and known in the fields, and the trees which have given them shelter, for them I know best. Now must I look again at the picture which an early artist has made of my patron Saint, my namesake, François, talking to the birds."

But, alas! money was very scarce. He felt out of place in the studios of most of the masters of Paris. Did they not look at him strangely, and call him the "man of the woods"? Yet they praised his work, which was so different from that of the others. In order to live, and now there was a wife and children to feed, Millet began to paint what would sell, however little the price. Not pictures from his mind and his dreams, but copies of artists he did not like but whom the gay people of Paris liked. Sometimes he drew title pages for songs, made signboards, and was even forced to give a picture in order to get a pair of shoes. Farther and farther away was he compelled to go from the kind of picture he wanted to paint: the Winnower, the Sower of Seed in the Fields, the Shepherdess tending her flocks. Discouraged, seeing his dreams fade farther and farther away, he remembered almost the last words of his father, who understood him and his desire to make truly beautiful pictures: "Never make an unworthy picture. Praise God by thought, by word and by deed."

He made up his mind, "Though life may be even harder and we suffer more, if you are willing we will leave this city where I and the pictures I want to make do not belong, and we will go to the village of Barbizon near to the great forest where God and Nature are not lost as they are here. There I can think and make with my fingers the pictures I see in my mind. They shall be worthy of my good father and of my grandmother, who encouraged me to paint the very best of my dreams. That I can promise you."

It had been a long journey, part of the way by cart and part of the way on foot. Tall and strong, broad of shoulder, dark gray-blue eyes looking expectantly ahead for the little village they had heard about so close to the deep woods, François Millet strode purposefully ahead, giving his two small and happy little daughters a ride over the long road, upon his strong, broad shoulders.

"Courage!" he called back to his wife, who more slowly followed him over the strange road, carrying their baby boy in her arms, her skirt raised to protect him from a heavy rain. "Our new home is before us, the village of Barbizon! And by the way some of our new neighbors look upon us, they take us for strolling players! But they shall see. François Millet will be able to paint true pictures and pictures of beauty here where there is plenty of space and air; where there are trees and birds and flowers, and the people who work in the soil. There is our new home—see it there before you—its tiled roof, jasmine and ivy covering its stone walls like my old home; the orchard where the young ones will play and I shall tell them stories of the flowers and the birds, and of good Saint Francis, just as my sainted grandmother used to tell me. That room with the high window shall be my workshop. The forest beyond shall be the school where I shall learn! Better this small cottage than a great palace in the crowded, noisy city."

There were the garden vegetables and flowers to tend in the morning, his pictures to paint in the afternoon. Then, when he was weary of working, the forest in which to rest and play with his children. Just as his father had taught him the beauties of the trees, the sky, the sunlight, so he taught them.

"I know no pleasures," he would say, "equal to that of lying on the ferns and looking at the clouds and the trees. I don't know what those rascals of trees say to one another, but they say something and we don't understand it, because we don't talk the same language, that is all! And the sun, how he freshens the greens and decks them with jewels after a shower!"

"Is it time now, Father," perhaps small François, his namesake, would eagerly ask, "for the story-pictures?"

"Yes, it is time for the Ogre with the long teeth, or for Jeanne, the Maid of our land who like yourselves played in the fields and the woods before she was called to save her country."

Then Millet would at once be surrounded by his boys and girls watching his skilful fingers bring alive before their very eyes their favorite stories.

The Sower swinging his right arm in rhythm with his steps as he scatters the seeds in the plowed land, the Gleaners bending their bodies, with beauty of line and of form, to search on the ground for corn and grain left after the wagon loads have taken the harvest from the golden field on that August day; the Angelus with its hard-working man and woman silhouetted in the last strong light of day, standing with bowed heads as the church bells chime; Springtime with its delicate blossoms, its yielding ground, its rainbow arching the sky; these are some of his pictures the whole world enjoys. Even as the artists who lived in the castle halls in the Middle Ages illuminated the calendar books of their masters with very real and beautiful pictures of everyday castle life, so did Jean François Millet illuminate by his pictures the simple everyday life of those who work in the fields. So did he show the beauty and poetry of the sun and shadow in the fields and the woods, true poems of Nature.

JAMES McNEILL WHISTLER

1834–1903

BEFORE THE STORY

JAMES ABBOTT McNEILL WHISTLER was a very unusual person. Many stories and criticisms have been written about him and his art, and his pictures will always be remembered because they, like their creator, are different.

He was born in Lowell, Massachusetts, although he once told a questioner who asked him his birthplace, "I never was born. I came from on high!" And the answer was, so the story goes, something like this, "What a mistake I have made. I should say you came from below!"

Whistler's father was George Washington Whistler, who was graduated from the United States Military Academy, and rose to the rank of major. But his lifework was that of civil engineer.

Both his father and his grandfather were musicians, the former also skilled in drawing. This heritage must have contributed a great deal to Whistler's love of beauty, skill in drawing, and musical interpretations of line and color.

When his father was made Consulting Engineer to the Imperial Russian Commission for building the first railway between Leningrad (St. Petersburg, as it was then) and Moscow, his mother went to join him, taking with her James and his brothers and sister.

Drawing lessons in Russia at the Imperial Academy of Fine Arts, visiting in London, and finally back to America, where he was sent to school at Pomfret, Connecticut—such was the early boyhood of Whistler.

Following the example of his father, James entered West Point as a cadet, where he excelled in drawing, but was dropped for poor work in chemistry!

Next followed an appointment as draughtsman in the United States Coast Survey in Washington, during which he received his first training in the process of etching. Little did he or his friends think then that he would acquire world-wide fame in that art, for his duties were to draw and etch plans and maps. Think what a fine training it must have been in accurate work! It was there in Washington that he began to show his genius in picture making, and soon chose that art for his profession.

Paris was the art center, so he determined to go there to study, a young man of twenty-one. After several years of study there, he went to London to live, but never recrossed the ocean to America.

James McNeill Whistler understood the beauty of simplicity and arrangement as did the artists of the East, and learned from the art of Japan which he understood and admired. He knew the importance of Nature, as they did, its tones and color harmonies. The story he told in his pictures was not so important to him as its expression.

The Thames River, winding its way through London, fascinated him, and he pictured it in its different moods. Some of them showed the river and its banks bathed in moonlight. He called those pictures nocturnes, a word with which we are familiar in music, and know, too, that it comes from the Latin word meaning "night."

Sometimes he showed the river at night bathed in a mist, as in his Battersea Bridge, which he called a "Nocturne in Blue and Silver." Another view of the bridge he called "Nocturne in Blue and Gold." Experimenting with his initials, J. M. W., he designed for his signature to these and other pictures a butterfly.

Best known of all is the portrait of his mother which, with his interest in decorative arrangement of line, tone, and color, he called an "Arrangement in Grey and Black." It is full of reality, however, and the sweet personality of his mother, and throughout the world it is known as a portrait of the painter's mother. More than that, it has come to stand for all mothers.

Very simple is the pose of the figure and the pattern of the picture, very beautiful and effective. Silhouetted against the lighter background of the room is the mother in a big, sweeping line. The picture on the wall with its dark border is in just the right place in the pattern, as is the curtain, distributing the dark notes in a pleasing harmony. In contrast are the light notes of the mother's cap, collar, cuffs, handkerchief, and the wall pictures. Again, and quite naturally, we use musical terms speaking of dark and light and color "notes." Simplicity, dignity, peace—are in this picture, portrayed with great tenderness and delicacy by the artist.

This famous "mother" portrait belongs to the French Government and when it was purchased, its creator, Whistler, was decorated with the Cross of the Legion of Honor. For many years it was in the Luxembourg Museum, in Paris, but it is now in the Louvre. It is the portrait which, in color prints, has been used to celebrate Mother's Day.

Some of Whistler's Pictures:

PORTRAIT OF THOMAS CARLYLE—Arrangement in Green and Grey
Corporation Gallery of Art, Glasgow

NOCTURNE IN BLUE AND GOLD—OLD BATTERSEA BRIDGE
National Gallery of British Art, London

NOCTURNE IN BLUE AND SILVER—BATTERSEA REACH
Freer Gallery, Washington

HARMONY IN YELLOW AND GOLD: THE GOLD GIRL, CONNIE GILCHRIST
Metropolitan Museum of Art, New York

CREMORNE GARDENS
Metropolitan Museum of Art, New York

THE WHITE GIRL
National Gallery of Art, Washington

ROSE AND SILVER: THE PRINCESS FROM THE LAND OF PORCELAIN
Freer Gallery, Washington

SELF PORTRAIT
Institute of Arts, Detroit

AN ARTIST WHO MADE HIS MOTHER FAMOUS: JAMES McNEILL WHISTLER

"Emma! Look at what Jimmie is doing!" gleefully whispered Willy. "Master Park will be after him!"

"Sh-h!" silenced his neighbor. "Teacher will hear you and look this way, and Jimmie won't be able to finish that picture! Wouldn't Doc be mad if he could see it?"

Bending low over his book sat young Jimmie Whistler, busy with his pencil. His delicate face was intent on the picture he was drawing on the book's margin. A lock of his dark hair bobbed gently up and down on his forehead, as he moved his head back and to the side a bit, from time to time, to better get the effect of the caricature he was making of the master.

"Think of it!" again whispered his brother, Willy, pride in his voice, "making a funny picture of Doctor Park! He's got courage, all right, my brother Jimmie has. Look! Doc is scowling, and looking this way!"

The master was surely gazing intently in that direction. From past experience he knew that Jimmie Whistler was a ringleader. Yet, he seemed to be studying his lesson, industriously enough. Hm! his pencil was most amazingly busy for a history lesson.

A sudden chuckle caught the master's ear. Another, and another, muffled by bent heads and discreetly applied hands and handkerchiefs, but unmistakably gleeful chuckles, yet so suddenly checked that he wondered if he could be imagining them. More and more sober and pensive became Jimmie Whistler's face, his soft curls giving him an almost angelic appearance. But more and more agitated grew the other boys' shoulders. No, he wasn't imagining it—they were bent almost double with heroically suppressed chuckles.

Swiftly the master acted. Before they could control their faces, he walked towards them, and noticed the laughter change quickly to dismay. Only Jimmie seemed undisturbed, paying no heed to the approaching teacher.

One glance over the boy's shoulder revealed a caricature of himself! It was so laughter-provoking that his own lips twitched and an appreciative twinkle appeared for an instant in his eyes. Covering it instantly with a very stern expression, he cried, "James Whistler, come with me!

"Hold out your hand, Sir!" he thundered, when he had him in the front of the room before the class, raising the ferule with a flourish.

"No! no! please, Sir!" begged Willy, "don't hurt Jimmie! I was laughing at his picture, and having fun, too. Jimmie just can't help making pictures. He didn't mean to insult you, Sir, only to make a funny picture!"

"No doubt, Master William, no doubt! But young James must be punished if he is going to make his pictures in school hours all over his lesson books. Hold out your hand, Sir!"

"I was urging Jimmie on!" cried another boy, running forward. "He's no worse than the rest of us. He's better 'cause he can draw! Let me take some of the feruling!"

"And me!" "Me, too!" "We were in it, just as much," cried the other boys, generously offering to take their share of the punishment.

"No doubt you all deserve to be feruled," sternly answered the master, "for disorder in school hours, but James is the leader, and he shall take the punishment today."

"Ah, Jamie," sighed his mother when Willy and he had told her of what had happened. "Are you going through life being a law unto yourself? You'll get into plenty of trouble, if you do."

"Poor Jamie," she laughed, as she talked with his father. "He's so generous and affectionate, and so sorry after he has cut up a caper. He's never sullen, like some boys, after he has been punished. But he's full of mischief, high-spirited, and chafes at binding rules.

"I sometimes wonder, George, just what our Jamie will

be when he grows up. He has your love of music and drawing, and his sense of rhythm sometimes shows itself in little poems, like the one he put under my plate at breakfast as a surprise on his last birthday. It's a beautiful little verse, and I shall always keep it. These gifts of his are for his amusement now, but I shouldn't wonder but what he will be an artist of some kind, one day. He's always making pictures of one kind or another. I don't believe any scolding words or Master Park's ferule will ever stop him!"

"Are we most there? Are we most there?" James and William and Deborah asked their mother for the thousandth time. The journey from Boston to Liverpool, on to Hamburg, then eastward by stage coach over very poor roads; and once more a journey by sea to Russia, was a tiresome one. Their father was building a railway in Russia between Moscow and St. Petersburg * for the Emperor, and he was anxiously awaiting them.

"Don't look so sad, Mother," begged Deborah as each put an arm around her when they neared their journey's end. "Please don't grieve any more for our baby brother. It makes us cry, too." On the long and fatiguing journey, the baby had died. "We'll be very good. See, Jimmie is drawing a picture, just for you."

"It's beautiful," declared Jimmie, as he watched the soft blue mists gather over a fascinating river in Russia, and the lights of the Russian capital city twinkling through it. "It is like beautiful music. If only it wasn't so cold. It makes me shiver! But, Mother—Father, please let me enter the Imperial Academy of Fine Arts right over

* *Now called Leningrad.*

there across the river! I can easily get there over that bridge of boats."

The cold of Russia did not agree with the delicate boy. Rheumatism and finally rheumatic fever attacked him, so that when his father announced a holiday in England he was delighted. He was quite proud, too, as were they all, for their father, Major Whistler, had been decorated with the Order of Saint Anne because of his success as an engineer.

"Yes," declared James, emphatically, when, after his return to Russia, he again suffered with rheumatic fever, "I'll be willing to stay in England with Deborah and her new doctor-husband, who likes to make pictures on copper plates, too! You and Father will soon be coming over again."

But Major Whistler died in Russia, from cholera, and his wife, Willy, and James traveled back to America.

James still sketched upon anything he had on hand—often a geography book in his Connecticut schoolroom. Geography was his favorite study since it gave him such a good chance to draw maps. And such maps! "They are wonderful!" the other scholars would cry. "How can you ever do it?"

"Are you sure you want to enter West Point as a cadet?" his mother asked him, anxiously.

"I'm sure, Mother. Wasn't Father born at Fort Wayne, and wasn't he on the staff at West Point? And wasn't Grandfather in the War of 1812? Though I don't expect I'm going to like all the military rules there!"

"Curly's a good fellow," the boys would say, "and can he draw? You should see his pictures. Why, he can make them any time. He's a good fellow, too, and strong, though he dresses sort of queer and wears his hair long. 'Curly'?

Why, that's the name we gave him because of the curl that hangs down over his forehead. Sure! he's a fighter! Why, once he licked a boy twice his size! Come on, Curly! steal out and get us something good to eat! You always have good luck. Then you can help us draw our maps!"

No, Whistler was not suited to a cadet's life. He was seldom on time, he didn't like the military discipline, and he didn't like chemistry! So, he and West Point parted, and the twenty-year-old boy went to Washington, called on Jefferson Davis, Secretary of War, and persuaded him to help him find something to do, still with the idea of a military career. Soon he was drawing and etching for the Coast Survey at a dollar and a half a day! And still he was late whenever he pleased, and still he spent a great deal of time drawing pictures, often upon the walls of his room!

"But, Jimmie," lamented his mother, when he returned to Connecticut, "I'm so disappointed. You must follow some career! George thinks that perhaps you would do well to become an engineer, like your father."

"I would, Mother, if I would make a good engineer. But I wouldn't. I've always liked to make pictures, so now I'm going to Paris to study art!"

While Whistler was having a good time in Paris with the other artists and writers there, he was studying the people, storing away pictures in his mind, later to be painted, and executing many there of the artist life around him. When he thought he had studied at his art long enough he decided that it was time for him to begin his career as a full-fledged painter, and that England might be a better place as a picture market than France. Besides, his family was there.

"I won't live with Deborah, but will set up a place for myself," he decided, "since Mother is coming to live with me; and William may come along later. And I'm going to have a house so close to the river that I can see it at any hour of the day and night.

"I'll picture it by sunlight, by moonlight, in clear weather and dimmed by a mist, just as the Japanese artists pictured their mountain in all kinds of weather. Mother will have to stand Japanese color-prints, fans, and screens all around her, for I want to fill myself with their beauty of line and tone and pattern, and simplicity, most of all. Beware! I shall soon be using all the members of my family as models. For I've decided to enlarge my scope and become a painter of portraits. What with etching and sketching and painting, I'll be more than busy.

"Dasha,* I'll paint you and young Annie together, and call it 'At the Piano,' and it shall have a background of gray and green and gold. The carpet shall be red and there must be a red covering on the table over there against the wall. We must have some dark notes, too. I have it! Your dress shall be black, also the violin case on the floor. Soft sunlight must be pouring into the room, shining upon the polished wood of the piano. Come, Dasha! Come, Annie! Let me pose you now. Can you keep still, Annie, and be patient? I'll tell you all about Paris, if you will."

"Now it's your turn, Mother," he declared one day. "I must capture you upon my canvas. Remember how, as a boy, I used to be always drawing a picture for you or writing a poem to give you as a surprise?"

"Indeed I do, Jimmie. And now my boy is a real artist, and going to make his old mother famous."

"Rather the other way around, Mother. You are going to make me famous. That's right, sit there so that I can paint you in profile. Sit just as you naturally would, Mother, just as I've seen you a thousand times, with your hands folded on your knees. See, I will arrange your cap

* *His step-sister, Deborah.*

strings—so! Hold your handkerchief a little less tightly to make a larger note of white, just there. Put your feet on this footstool, which will make you more comfortable and break the floor line in just the right place. You see, Mother, I'll have to do the talking, for I want you to keep that expression, so peaceful, so kind. Ah, Mother, I wonder if I can do you justice?"

For a few moments Whistler busied himself with mixing his colors on a table nearby, the tones he would need for flesh, dress, floor, and background. And such large and long brushes he used! He liked to cover the whole canvas at one sitting, and then do it over again and again at other sittings.

"This long, sweeping line is graceful, the colors are few and simple—just an arrangement in gray and black. Wait a moment, until I straighten that picture which is hung in exactly the right spot. Ah, this will be lovely in tone and pattern, a picture that the great Velazquez of Spain might be willing to claim.

"Now that you, Mother, the curtain, pictures, and footstool are all in the right places for the pattern of the whole, and the light just soft enough, I'll begin. Quick-tempered I may be and ready for combat—but what else can you expect with my fighting ancestry?—and deserving the limerick written about me, which begins, 'There's a combative artist named Whistler'; yet I have a message for the world in my pictures, and something tells me that this one, the portrait of my mother, will be the most loved and the best known."

WINSLOW HOMER

1836–1910

BEFORE THE STORY

THE EARTH, the Sky, and the Sea! Brown and blue and green, and all the other colors flashing across them. Perhaps most marvelous of all is the sea, and none knows it more than

"They that go down to the seas in ships, that do business in great waters:
These see the works of the Lord, and his wonders in the deep.
For he commandeth, and raiseth the stormy wind, which lifteth up the waves thereof,
They mount up to the heaven, they go down again to the depths;

. . . . . .

He maketh the storm a calm, so that the waves thereof are still." *

Next to them, painters of the sea have the eyes to behold its strength, its everchanging color and its everlasting glory. They have eyes to see and the hearts to understand.

They, too, know the joy of fine weather, the sunlight warming the golden sands, the salt-laden breeze blowing across their faces, the mystery of fogs, the rhythm of the ever-moving waves, the power and strength of the great waters, the sound of the surf pounding upon the rocks, the fullness of color ever changing with the day, the maj-

* *From Psalm 107.*

esty of the vast ocean! They, too, these painters of the sea, know "Sea Fever."

"I must down to the seas again, to the lonely sea and the sky,
And all I ask is a tall ship and a star to steer her by,
And the wheel's kick and the wind's song and the white sail's
 shaking,
And a gray mist on the sea's face and a gray dawn breaking." *

So, I think, felt the greatest of our American painters of the sea, Winslow Homer.

No doubt Winslow Homer inherited his love of the sea from Captain John Homer, one of his ancestors, who sailed to America from England in his own little ship in the middle of the seventeenth century, and settled in Boston. There were other seagoing relatives, too, so you see Winslow came quite naturally by his love for it.

He was born in 1836, and when he was six years old, his family moved to Cambridge, Massachusetts, where Winslow was sent to school. There he often spent his time in drawing with his pencil or crayon upon a page of his schoolbook, when he should have been learning his lessons. You can imagine the scoldings which broke over his daydreaming head! Although his father did not, of course, uphold this neglect of his lessons and making of drawings in his schoolbooks, yet he did sympathize with his boy's desire to learn to paint, which is a relief to know, I am sure, for so often we read in the lives of artists that their parents or parent had other plans upon which they insisted.

From the very first Winslow Homer liked to make pictures of the out-of-doors, where he had a good time fishing and playing with his animal friends. When he

* *From John Masefield's "Salt-Water Ballads."*

reached his eighteenth birthday and school was behind him, his father suggested that he learn engraving as a beginning to his career. Accordingly, he was apprenticed to a lithographer in Boston, and when his two years of apprenticeship were over, and his work so well done that a New York publishing house offered him a similar position, on his twenty-first birthday he set up in his own studio as an illustrator, and was delighted when his drawings were accepted by Ballou's *Pictorial Monthly* of Boston, and *Harper's Weekly* of New York.

When Winslow Homer was twenty-three years of age he went to New York, where he studied painting with a French artist and attended a night class in the National Academy of Design, the only painting lessons he ever had!

Then came the Civil War with great excitement everywhere and the newspapers made hurried preparations to send their men to the front. *Harper's Weekly* had illustrations of each week's events, and having noticed Winslow Homer's work in Boston so favorably that they had previously offered him a position, sent for him again to go to Washington as their special artist to make illustrations of Lincoln's inauguration, and to go to the front to get pictures of the soldier life in McClellan's army. He crossed the Potomac with the first regiment of volunteers in 1861. Some of the sketches he made, he used as subjects for his first pictures, such as "Rations," "The Bright Side," and "Prisoners from the Front," all of them true to life, and full of character, showing his wonderful truth of observation. Because of these timely pictures appealing to so many who had relatives and friends at the front, especially his "Prisoners from the Front," which, by the way, you can see in the Metropolitan Museum of Art, New York, he was made a member of the Academy.

Winslow Homer was nearly fifty years old before he

began his pictures dealing with the ocean in all of its moods, and the life of sailors and fishermen. For two years, he stayed among the fisherfolk near Newcastle, in England, and learned to understand the mystery of the sea, its might and majesty, its perils in storm as well as its joys in fair weather.

In 1884, when he was forty-eight years of age, he made his home on the Maine shore where he painted those later pictures of the sea and the folk who live by the sea, which brought him fame. When the winter weather was too bad, he went to Florida or the Bahamas and painted water color sketches glowing in color. Then back again to Maine by March of each year until, at his death in 1910 he had become famous as the interpreter of the Maine Coast.

Winslow Homer knew just what stories of the sea and the fishermen he wanted to tell, and just how to tell them. Nature was his teacher, and he caught the simple truth of what he observed, and made those who look at his canvases see it, too. "Talent!" he said. "There is no such thing as talent. What they call talent is nothing but the capacity for doing continuous hard work in the right way."

Such dramatic pictures of the moods of the sea he has left us—the weight and bulk of the water, the movement and force of the incoming waves, even the sound of a northeast storm!

Some of Homer's Pictures

MOONLIGHT—WOOD'S ISLAND LIGHT
Metropolitan Museum of Art, New York
THE GULF STREAM
Metropolitan Museum of Art, New York

Maine Coast
Metropolitan Museum of Art, New York
Northeaster
Metropolitan Museum of Art, New York
High Cliff, Coast of Maine
National Gallery of Art, Washington
Breezing Up
National Gallery of Art, Washington
The Fox Hunt
Pennsylvania Academy of the Fine Arts, Philadelphia
Watching the Breakers
Art Institute, Chicago
The Gale
Worcester Art Museum, Worcester
The Wreck
Carnegie Institute, Pittsburgh
Cannon Rock
Metropolitan Museum of Art, New York
Fog Warning
Museum of Fine Arts, Boston

THE SONG OF THE SEA: WINSLOW HOMER

"Come, Sam! come!" and Sam, a faithful Irish terrier, Winslow Homer's constant companion for over ten years, came bounding to join his master and his master's nephews, Arthur and Charlie. What better fun could there be than a day with Uncle Winslow, who could tell such marvelous stories, when he had a mind, and who could paint such grand pictures? Not every boy had an uncle who could capture the very ocean and put it upon his canvas until you could almost feel the wet spray! No, sir! And nobody else at Prout's Neck, or in the whole state of Maine, had an uncle who could make little pictures of them—just as *easy!*

Often they would look at the funny drawings made of themselves when they were much younger, just small boys. "Look at Arthur lifting his foot to step over an angleworm so he won't hurt it!" Charlie would point out in high glee. "Look at Charlie sitting right down on top of poor old puss and pulling Sam's tail!" Arthur would come back at him, in high amusement. But neither could deny that the other looked "just as real!" Besides, one day Uncle Winslow had shown them some sketches he had made when he was just a boy like themselves.

"Guess he didn't always study his geography lesson!" chuckled Arthur. "Look, Charlie, at the queer maps he has drawn on the margin and in the back of the books! And in that reader is a picture of a pretty real-looking boy!"

"Bet he had to stay in after school for marking up his books," murmured Charlie. "Didn't you, Uncle Winslow?" But Uncle Winslow had only winked at them and smiled and shown them a drawing he had made when only eleven. "Just think of it!" breathed Charlie, with popping eyes, as he looked at the sketch.

It was called "The Beetle and Wedge," and there were four boys, no bigger and no older than they, playing a rather strange game. One boy was taking the part of the wedge, another of the beetle, and the other two were working hard to make the beetle and the wedge collide!

"And who do you suppose the hapless beetle is?" asked Uncle Homer, quite solemnly. The two boys looked again at the drawing of the small boy, his arms and legs spread out and securely held by the two other boys who were going to swing him with a great deal of force against the back of the boy who was taking the part of the wedge and who was waiting, braced upon all fours, on the grass. Those figures were drawn as though actually playing the game, and both Charlie and Arthur wondered how any eleven-year-old boy could make such a natural-looking picture. But neither of them had any idea who the boy taking the part of the beetle might be. They shook their heads. "Who is the boy?" they asked.

Winslow Homer smiled. "The boy who is taking the part of the unfortunate beetle," he said, "is Arthur Homer, your father!"

Of course, they liked to go fishing with their uncle and to take hikes with him and loyal old Sam.

One day when they were walking, Sam began to bark and so, before they could see him or hear him, they knew a stranger was near.

He was a very finely dressed man, quite different from the folk of Prout's Neck, so Charlie and Arthur thought perhaps he had come from the city. Sam decided he looked quite respectable, and stopped his barking. Straight up to them he walked, looked up and down Uncle Winslow's old, rough suit, felt hat all out of shape, high rubber boots, and the fishing-rod which was almost as constant a companion on his walks as his terrier, Sam. Then he said:

"I say, my man, if you can tell me where I can find Winslow Homer, I have a quarter here for you." *

The roughly dressed man in fisherman's clothes replied, "Where's your quarter?"

Rather enviously, Charlie and Arthur watched that quarter handed over. Then they heard their uncle say, "I am Winslow Homer!"

* *See Mr. Downe's "Life of Homer."*

How they all laughed, the man from the city too.

When no one else was around, the boys were permitted to ask questions if they wished, to talk, and to watch their uncle at work. Sometimes, if they were very quiet, he let them go with him into a funny little house which could be moved from one place to another, and which was very convenient in the time of a storm. That was their goal today as they started out. The boys had made up their minds to ask Uncle Winslow about something they had heard of him down in the village, and Arthur ventured, "Did you really see Abraham Lincoln, Uncle Winslow?"

They had to wait for some time for a reply, patiently suiting or trying to suit their shorter steps to their uncle's longer ones, Sam running on ahead, giving a few short barks as if to say, "Hurry up, comrades! a storm is coming, so let's get to shelter!" They were used to Uncle Winslow's silences and knew that he would not forget to answer in good time. The wind was already blowing into a gale so that they had to listen very closely when he did begin to speak, else the words would have gone floating off, perhaps out to sea!

"It was in '61 that I was sent out to the seat of war by *Harper's Weekly* as artist-correspondent. That means that I was to draw pictures just as I have drawn pictures of you, and send them back to be published in the magazine. Before I went to the place where they were fighting to save the Union and free the slaves, I went to Washington and made some pictures of Abraham Lincoln taking the solemn oath of the office of President of the United States, and of the grand procession in honor of it. Great crowds of eager people were gathered to hear him read his speech as he stood in the portico of the Capitol, surrounded by high officers of state, and gazing with so kind and brotherly a look at all the people who had gathered."

"As if he loved them all?" ventured Arthur, the older boy, who had often heard stories and seen pictures of the great-hearted, plain, kindly man who had brought the terrible war to a close. It made them very proud to think that their Uncle Winslow had made pictures of him.

"As if he loved them all, which he truly did. How the cannon thundered and the people shouted after Abraham Lincoln earnestly said, his hand upon the Bible: 'I, Abraham Lincoln, do solemnly swear that I will faithfully execute the office of President of the United States, and will, to the best of my ability, preserve, protect, and defend the Constitution of the United States.' "

The surf was pounding upon the high cliffs with such a thundering, as they drew nearer, that the boys had to cup their hands to their mouths as they spoke. The wind blew so that they kept very close to their uncle's side. The louder the pounding of the surf, the more violent the wind, the more excited grew Sam! For he loved the sight of the sea and its sound, the feel of the wind, just as did his master. They could now see the little house down on the rocks. Soon they would be within its shelter.

"Did you get to where the boys in the blue and the gray were really fighting?" shouted Arthur, ardently. An uncle who had been right on the battlefront, and had made pictures of the soldiers—that was an uncle worth having indeed!

"To the front with the first volunteers; and I painted dozens of soldier pictures. You shall see some of them one day, for most of them came out in *Harper's Weekly*. Soldiers singing, 'John Brown's Body'; soldiers playing cards by the campfire, with the moon peeping out from behind the clouds; 'Prisoners from the Front'; the Army of the Potomac, marching and fighting and camping; a bayonet charge; 'Rations,' showing the hardships at camp;

'Bright Side,' with some colored teamsters resting in the sunlight at the side of their tent; 'Home Sweet Home.' Ever so many of them. But here we are. Take tight hold of me, heads down to the wind, and follow Sam, who is making for shelter!"

They were in the little movable painting house which Winslow Homer had ordered built, set on runners, so that it could be moved wherever he wished, and thus give him a chance to paint his dearly loved sea even in the cold and stormy weather. Directly opposite them, as they pushed open the door and banged it shut against the force of the wind, was a big plate-glass window. "The Magic Window," the boys had named it on the rare visits when they had been allowed to look out at the picture of the great sea framed in by it, and watched their uncle transfer it to his canvas. Out upon the rocks the little house with its "magic window" had been placed that day, the sea tumbling and frothing below, the wind shaking it. The white tops of the breakers sometimes looked as if they were going to soar up above their very heads, and the snowy spray dashed against the cliffs and pounded furiously upon the snug little shelter, as if bent on gaining entrance.

"A regular Northeaster!" exulted their uncle, as the boys flattened themselves into the corner, for well they knew they would not be allowed to stay if he should find them in the way. Sam, who was so well trained that he was often allowed to stay with his master in the strange little house, stood upon his hind paws, gently resting his front paws upon the very edge of the big window, and like his master gazed far out over the stormy waters reflecting the leaden storm clouds in the sky.

"Just the way I want it!" exulted the artist again, paying no heed to the wide-eyed boys and the watchful, quiet dog. "A rare day, with old ocean in full action and in a savage mood, and I, standing on the shore of this loud sounding sea, about to capture a bit of its power, its sound, its color and its motion!"

On came the great waves breaking upon the high, dark cliffs, drenching them and being drawn back into the seething bed of the ocean. Up tossed the lace-like spray, up above the cliffs, slapping the snug little house and sprinkling it as it broke into thousands of little drops. Quiet and motionless for a while, stood Winslow Homer, waiting for the storm to reach just the height of its fury which he, with palette and brushes and color ready, was waiting to make last upon his canvas. Equally quiet were Arthur and Charlie, watching with fascinated eyes the storm which beat against their magic window, and wondering when Uncle Winslow was going to begin. Equally quiet was Sam. He was quite used to his master's ways.

Big waves and mighty waves, tossing,
thundering sea!
Gray and green and snowy white the
changeful patterns be.
Onward and forward, sweeping towards
the shore.
Upward and skyward with a threatening
roar!
The wind's in the water, the wind's in
the sky,
The spray sweeps the rocky coast till
not a spot is dry.
There's power in the ocean, there's majesty
and pride.
There's grace in the curving waves a-hasten-
ing on the tide.
There's a pattern of color, and a snowy lace-
like foam.
If I can't be on the ocean, close by I'll make
my home!

Perhaps something like this was singing in Winslow Homer's mind. He was never going to leave his home on the rocky coast of Maine except for the few winter months when the bitter cold and the savage tempests drove him away. Always, so long as he lived, he would come back.

At last the storm reached the height for which the painter was waiting. Quickly he made ready his palette with the storm colors which he could so easily see through his great window. Quickly and firmly he grasped his brushes and began to paint the storm of gray and green upon the moving waters, with notes of white crashing through at the crests of the waves, and the dull gray storm sky reflecting itself in the sea.

"Ah! here comes a giant wave! nearer, nearer, growing more strong and mighty with every passing second and every fresh gale of wind. How heavy it looks, as if it would never change, and yet soon it will break into its pattern of foam, and fall, to rise again! I have it blocked in now, imprisoned, to be perfected and finished later, with its seething and everchanging pattern of foam upon its swelling side, white against the cold blending of blue and green beneath. That is what I see before me. The roar of the sea and the wind in the storm, and the great wall of foam and spray beating upon the ledge at the left, that is what I hear. Both belong to the picture of this stormy day, which I shall call 'The Northeaster.' "

"Are you not afraid of the storm and the wind?" asked small Charlie, rather awed by the violence of the wind and the waves.

"Did not Captain John Homer sail from England across the Atlantic, often rougher than you see it today, in his own little ship over two hundred years ago? And have I not found a pirate ancestor up our family tree? No, I love the mighty sea in its stormiest, roughest mood; and the salt spray flying!"

The light, with the northeast storm raging, soon waned. The painter placed securely against the wall his picture, the single motion of that oncoming wave in a threatening sea, with the leaden sky overhead, so quickly and powerfully painted. The finishing touches by those brushes held so surely, could wait.

"It looks just the way the stormy sea did out of our Magic Window!" cried Charlie. "And you can almost hear the pounding of the painted waves!" added Arthur, lifting admiring eyes to his uncle's face. Sam gave a little yelp of delight. He, too, knew that the painter was through working for that day. He licked his master's hand.

It was even more difficult to get home than it had been to go down the rocks to the little house with the Magic Window. The boys clung to their uncle's hand. Even Sam held his head down, buffeting the wind. But the painter's head was up, flung back to the full force of the wind and the spray.

"Have you any unmade pictures tucked away in your mind, waiting to be painted, Uncle Winslow?" asked Arthur. He had heard one of the village folk say that when Winslow Homer, the painter-man, was unusually quiet, he was busy with his dream pictures which he was painting in his mind, one day to put them in color upon his canvas.

"Plenty of them, all pictures of the sea, and just waiting for old ocean to be in the right moods. Did you ever notice how very changeable she is?"

"Tell us some of them," begged both boys together. "The ones you think you will like the best! There is time for at least two or three word pictures before we get home, and the wind isn't roaring and whistling quite so hard; so we can hear. Tell us the ones you want to paint the most!"

The painter thought for a moment, his eyes seeming to look afar off. But both the boys knew that their painter-uncle was seeing just then with the eyes of his mind. They had seen that look before.

"Some day, and soon, after a bad storm at sea, which has roughened the waters, I shall paint Cannon Rock dark against the lighter waters, and an incoming wave breaking and swirling, another one hurrying after it and spilling its foam at the top, about to churn and boom like its neighbor. Perhaps once more I shall paint the moonlight on the waters, as I did last year."

"I know," cried Arthur, "I've seen it, and I remember that summer night when the moonlight made a wide silvery path across the water. It was all so peaceful and calm. And you, Uncle, jumped up from your smoking and said, 'I've got an idea! Good night, Arthur!' and ran to get your painting things and hurried down to the rocks close to the shore!"

"There I worked without stopping until one o'clock the next morning, and painted my picture by the clear, silver light of that glorious moon! And off in the distance at the right, I made the red eye of Wood Island Light always twinkling through the night to warn the sailors. . . .

"Or, perhaps I shall paint a great ship's bell, and the head of a rugged sailor looking up at the starry sky, while over the rail of the ship a great wave is breaking into white foam, as he calls out 'All's Well!' One day I shall picture a coming storm with fisher folk standing upon the dark rocks, silhouetted against the lighter sky and the sea, the wind whipping their clothes as they watch. Early morning with the sun just rising after a storm has freshened the clear colors of the waves and made more snowy white their crests of foam; the high cliffs, a long line of them, with the waves breaking upon them, and the surf dashing and pounding against them; sunset with a storm gathering; a wreck at sea, with the men on the shore, heroes all of them, as they do their work of getting out the lifeboats and venturing into the mountainous sea. A hundred pictures come to me which will show the beauty of our rugged, rocky coast; the might, the splendor, and yet the mystery of the sea, its ever different colors in the changing lights of day and night, the fogs and the mists, the graceful motion of the incoming waves, the sparkle of the light upon the ocean, the sound of surf and wind, all the majesty of the vast sea."

"And I have loved thee, Ocean!
. . . from a boy
I wantoned with thy breakers, . . .
And trusted to thy billows far and near,
And laid my hand upon thy mane—as I do here." *

* *Lord Byron's "Man and Nature."*

EDWIN AUSTIN ABBEY

1852–1911

BEFORE THE STORY

There are few boys and girls in this country or across the sea who do not know the story of King Arthur and his knights. I should have said stories, for there are many of them. A long, long time ago, before the days of King Richard of the Lionheart in England, about eight hundred years ago, the name of King Arthur first found its way into English literature. A man named Geoffrey of Monmouth told the stories of the ancient British King Arthur, in his History of the Britons. Sir Thomas Malory, who lived at the time of Edward the Fourth, nearly five hundred years ago, translated them from the Latin into English. William Caxton, the first English printer, printed them.

The stories enchanted grown men and women at the courts of kings in Europe during the Middle Ages and have continued to be told and retold for the pleasure of boys and girls and grown-ups right up to the twentieth century!

Artists have told the stories in pictures without words, but no artist has told them so truthfully and so beautifully as Edwin Austin Abbey, who won for himself the title of "The Painter of the Past."

Edwin Abbey was a painter of many pictures—but best of all he liked to bring alive some bygone story. He it is, who more than any other artist, perhaps more than any writer of the stories, has made vivid for us King Arthur's Court.

Edwin Abbey was born in 1852 in Philadelphia and like all the other famous artists we have read about in this book, began to draw when he was very young. He became a magazine illustrator and when he was twenty-eight, went to England to live. He loved to paint English scenes and characters. Keen observation, a vivid imagination and patient, hard work, soon made him one of the best illustrators of his time, and there was not a detail of costume or setting that he did not know.

The same year, 1890, in which his first oil painting was accepted by the Royal Academy, he was asked to decorate the walls of a room in the Boston Public Library, and produced his great series of the Quest of the Holy Grail. So Edwin Austin Abbey became the painter of murals as well as the illustrator.

He died in England in 1911, where he had been knighted by King Edward VII after painting his coronation ceremony.

I do hope that all of you will go to the Boston Public Library to see the panels representing the Grail story, so interesting and dramatic, so full of decoration, so simple in treatment, so glowing in color. Mr. Abbey has been said to have interpreted the soul of the Legend of the Holy Grail.

Some of Abbey's Works:

THE QUEST OF THE HOLY GRAIL (*murals*)
Public Library, Boston

MURALS IN THE PENNSYLVANIA STATE CAPITOL, HARRISBURG
Religion—Science—Law
Penn's Treaty with the Indians
Reading of the Declaration of Independence
KING LEAR
Metropolitan Museum of Art, New York
THE DIRGE OF THE THREE QUEENS (*pastel*)
Metropolitan Museum of Art, New York

EDWIN AUSTIN ABBEY, WHO PICTURED KING ARTHUR'S COURT

A cozy room in a Philadelphia home with a two-year-old boy in a high chair, making strange marks with a pencil upon scraps of paper which a small girl kept supplying. "I do believe Ned is making pictures of omnibuses!" she declared, after she had frantically found a tenth scrap of paper for the imperious and strangely insistent baby, who waved his pencil—painstakingly sharpened for him a dozen times—and by his expression and the tones of his voice, made it quite clear that he would allow no one and nothing to interfere with his artistic career!

"It may well be, Emma, that Ned is drawing pictures of omnibuses," answered Mrs. Abbey complacently, keeping on busily with her embroidery. "His father wants him to grow up into the finest doctor or lawyer in the country; but I would be content if he should be a minister, a writer, or even a painter of pictures. He could do a great deal of good at whichever profession he chooses. He does enjoy the feel of a pencil in his chubby hand. Look at him, Emma! The determination with which the child is making his first pictures! Who knows but what he will make the name of Abbey famous, one day! But we need not worry our heads about it yet awhile, Emma. First of all, he must learn to be kind and obedient."

So obedient did Ned become under his mother's training, that he was something of a martyr one day. "My Ned must not be so dainty with his food! He must not pick and choose, but eat what is placed before him. There are many hungry boys in the world who would be only too glad and grateful for what you have. So, Ned must remember his manners and eat what is given him."

So deeply did "Ned" Abbey take this to heart, that the next time he went with his mother to visit some relatives, he determined to remember his manners at all costs! A glass of milk was placed before him. All unknown to the hostess, or to his mother, a fly had dipped into it and was frantically struggling to get out! Ned looked appealingly at his mother, but she was busy talking with the grown-ups. Quite unconscious of his appeal, but observing that he was being what she considered "too dainty with his food," she gave him a little nudge, glancing meaningly in the direction of the glass of milk which he had not touched. "Drink your milk, Ned!" she admonished him.

Poor Ned gave one more despairing glance at his mother, who was again busy talking and heeded him not at all; one more agonized glance at his glass of milk in which the fly was still a prisoner. Then he dutifully drank down that milk, fly and all!

It was hard to put his mind on his lessons at school, when a great civil war was breaking over the land. Thoughts of the soldier boys must have appeared often between his eyes and the printed pages of his books; pictures of them upon the pages. Sometimes long thoughts of knights who fought in tourneys, with fair ladies watching them and cheering them on to victory, came to him and pictures of those knights in shining armor appeared before him. These were much more interesting to him than what was set before him to learn.

"Well, my son," his father would often inquire, "how do your lessons go in school? It is well to begin early to study towards one's profession. Which shall it be, Ned, a doctor or a lawyer? Or perhaps a minister? Any one of the three would well please your mother and myself."

Edwin hesitated. No doubt he hesitated a long time, for he had no wish to bring unhappiness to his mother and father, who were so kind to him. But the professions his father mentioned did not at all appeal to him. They had nothing to do with the people he could make live again—just by calling them forth in his fancy, and then capturing them upon his paper.

"I can draw better than anything else, Father," the boy timidly suggested. "Could I not study painting?"

They compromised. Edwin should have lessons in drawing at the Pennsylvania Academy of Fine Arts, but he must also learn a trade, for his father had little faith that a painter of pictures would be able to earn his bread and butter. How about the printer's trade? his father thought. It would keep the boy's fingers busy and might lead to a publisher's profession. Perhaps he would get over his desire to become an artist.

Edwin, or Ned as he was called, began as a printer's "devil" on a Philadelphia paper, having plenty of jobs to keep his inky fingers busy! The next step was typesetting, and every week he took lessons in drawing and every night he sketched the people he had seen during the day and those who came to his fancy.

"How about *Harper's Weekly?*" his employer asked one day, seeing that the boy was a real artist. Then Ned's eyes sparkled. That was far more to his liking.

"The same paper that sent Mr. Winslow Homer to the front!" he exulted, for he greatly admired that artist. Thus Edwin Abbey's art career began.

"The more a man knows, the longer it takes you to find out how much he knows," he often used to say. Every day he worked hard to make his ambitions come true. It was his will, his courage, and his own hard work, with the willingness to take infinite pains, which enabled him to realize the fulfillment of the dreams he had as a boy making drawings of the pictures which filled his mind.

Many are the poems and stories he illustrated, among them stories from Dickens and Shakespeare. But perhaps he is best known by his picture stories of King Arthur and his Court which decorate one of the rooms in the Boston Public Library. There, he showed "his worship of Truth by discerning the Beautiful in all things." * Each part of the story is simply told, pleasing in its decoration, its beauty of form, of color, and harmony of design, as each is related to the other.

It was in England that he planned the stories into a series of pictures, in which the figure of the perfect knight, Sir Galahad, in his scarlet robe or tunic, is seen again and again, all the way around the room, that note of color holding the many pictures together.

Up early in the morning, he worked hard at his canvases throughout the day—now stopping to sketch again and again until he had perfected it; a hand, a foot, and the expression of a face. Costumes, too, played an important part in his pictures and Edwin Abbey was ready to take all the pains in the world to make his picture stories correct in their costumes and setting. Rare tapestries adorned

* *From a speech in his honor when he was being given the honorary degree of Doctor of Laws by the University of Pennsylvania.*

the walls of his studio; suits of chain armor stood waiting to protect brave knights who went dauntlessly forth to seek adventure; silks, velvets, and satins were ready to enclose in graceful folds the fair ladies of the court of some ancient king.

What joy must have possessed the painter when the procession of picture stories was finished! It was the work of many years. What satisfaction he must have felt when he received a letter from the President of the Trustees of the Boston Public Library, telling of the Resolution passed, on July 14th, 1902.

"The Trustees of the Boston Public Library desire to express to Mr. Edwin A. Abbey, upon the completion of his work for their institution, their great satisfaction with the subject he has chosen, and the attractive manner in which it has been executed. They hope that the fine results of Mr. Abbey's genius in making so beautiful this room of the Library by the representation of a romance dear to the poetical and religious heart of Christendom may open new fields to his gifts, and in these days of engrossing outward activities, lead many, by the enjoyment of this painting, to some deeper and more generous interest in Art and Literature."

This is the story which the artist has told in color upon the library walls. It moves as simply and dramatically in its action, as in its writing or telling by those who made it live in kings' courts. Almost like a tapestry of figures it seems, decorating the walls.

The baby, Galahad, son of the brave knight Launcelot and the fair Elaine, laughed with delight as he reached up his chubby hands toward the Holy Cup, veiled with red, which was shown to him by the Angel of the Grail, a radiant light flooding her face and white garments. Eagerly he looked towards that sacred emblem which was to guard and make beautiful his life. As he grew older, he heard about the Holy Cup—the glimpse of which he received as a baby was only a dream to him—and like the other brave knights, longed to reach the castle of Amfortas, who had been made leader of the Knights of the Grail. 'Twas said that he had sinned and because of it, he and his court were cast under a spell in his castle, and could only be released at the coming of a knight so pure in body, in thought, and in deed, that he could look upon the Holy Cup.

"May I be that brave and pure knight!" prayed Galahad often, as cared for by the nuns into whose safe keeping he was given as a baby, he dreamed of the time to come when he should receive the accolade of knighthood, and join the other knights in the glorious Quest.

"Kneel before the altar of our chapel, the whole night through," counseled the nuns of the Abbey, close on to his fifteenth birthday. "We have sent for Sir Launcelot to knight thee on the morrow."

At the foot of the altar through the hours of the night Galahad kept vigil, clad in his robe of scarlet. With the morrow appeared Sir Launcelot and another knight from King Arthur's court, and knelt behind him in the presence of the nuns of the Abbey, reverently holding their lighted tapers, to buckle upon his heels the golden spurs.

"God help you to maintain your vow, Sir Galahad," earnestly counseled Sir Launcelot after he had given the accolade of knighthood. "May you be true to your high pledge of speaking the truth, maintaining the right, protecting the poor and oppressed and all women who are distressed, and being kind, courteous, and chivalrous to all. May you at all times honor the true God."

As the newly made knight, Sir Galahad, still knelt before the altar, he vaguely remembered the glory of the cup he had seen as a babe, but he knew not whether he had dreamed it.

A high feast was set at King Arthur's court at Camelot. The knights had taken their seats at the King's Round Table, till all places were filled save one, The Siege Perilous, where only the perfect knight might sit.

The steward had served them, when the great hall grew greatly darkened, and before them appeared a holy man, clothed in white. By the hand he slowly led a young knight, clad in a crimson robe, without sword or shield.

"Sire," the old man addressed King Arthur, "behold this young knight of the lineage of kings, who brings to you great marvels on this day."

"You and the young knight are right truly welcome," answered King Arthur. "You shall be served straightway."

To the amazement of those assembled in the great hall, the old, white-robed man led the young knight to the Siege Perilous. He lifted up the crimson cloth which covered it and found upon it letters which read, "This is the siege of Galahad the high prince."

A sigh of awe went up throughout the great hall when the young knight, Galahad, sat upon the seat where none had ventured to sit before. Sir Launcelot, who sat near by, beheld him whom he had knighted and recognized him as his son, and rejoiced that he would be the pure knight who should see the Holy Grail. The sword-hilts of all the knights, held high, gave throughout the hall the sign of the cross.

"Welcome, Sir Galahad," cried King Arthur. "You shall lead my true knights in the search for the Holy Grail!"

One hundred and fifty knights, all of the Table Round, were ready to start out. They gathered in the cathedral in their armor, their gay banners and lances held high as they knelt for the bishop to bless them before they started out upon their perilous quest. King Arthur, his Queen, those of the court and the poorest in the kingdom as well, wept as they saw them go their perilous ways.

Not far had Sir Galahad ridden before he came upon a strong castle, the Castle of the Grail. There in the great hall King Amfortas, its guardian, lay upon his couch, his whole court like himself waiting for the knight who was destined to break the spell which held them. Although Sir Galahad saw passing beyond the sleeping king the glorious Procession of the Grail, he failed to ask the question of its meaning, thinking to solve the mystery himself. And the King and his court still slept.

But half a mile had Sir Galahad ridden when he saw in a valley before him another strong castle beside a bright river.

"Fair Sir," a very old man informed him, "this is the Castle of the Maidens."

Sorrowing, for he had not only been unable to lift the spell from the Castle of the Grail but from the three maidens he met by the roadside on the way thither, he entered the Castle of the Maidens, though the old man had counseled him against it, because of the evil to be encountered within.

There, Sir Galahad met seven captive maidens imprisoned by Seven Knights of Darkness, with all of whom he fought till they fled. Sword struck sword, and scaly armor heavily clashed upon protecting shields ere the Good Knight was victorious. Thereupon was delivered to him by a holy man at the inner gate of the castle, the castle's keys. "Sir, take you the keys to this castle!" Whereupon, Sir Galahad opened the gates and passed swiftly within.

Many people greeted him. "Sir, ye be welcome, for long

have we awaited here our deliverance."

"Welcome, brave Knight!" cried the seven goodly maidens he had freed. "Long have we waited for your coming! Now are you closer to the Holy Grail."

After overcoming the Evil Knights and thus rescuing the Virtuous Maidens, Sir Galahad once again reached the Castle of the Grail, which before he had failed to free from its spell. Again, he failed to understand the meaning of the sleeping King and court, and the procession of the Grail, covered from his eyes, which was borne before him.

"Oh, King," he cried in compassion, on his knees before him, "what aileth thee? What meaneth these mysteries?" Forthwith, at his question of sympathy, Light and Life glowed throughout the castle; the King, the Knights, the Maidens lived, as the Angel of the Grail bore the healing cup away.

All the land round about the castle, as well as those within, had been freed from the wickedness which had blighted and darkened it, as Sir Galahad in his bright red mantle, holding his lance with his red and white banner floating from it, rode away upon his snow-white horse to his last great adventure—the finding and the seeing of the Holy Grail.

After three days of riding, Sir Galahad came to the shore of the sea and there was a ship waiting, with two other brave knights of King Arthur's court. King Solomon's ship it was, the ship of Wisdom, which bore them in safety across the dark and stormy waters, and guiding the ship to safety, was the Guardian of the Grail. The city of Sarras they reached, with its towers reaching skyward along the edge of the water. There they helped to heal the sick, but were imprisoned by the wicked King, until he, too, fell ill and sent for the knights to implore their mercy. Then was Galahad made King of the city.

There, for the first time, the Grail was seen, unveiled, by Sir Galahad. "Galahad!" a voice cried. "Now shalt thou see that which thou hast come so far to see; which only the pure and perfect knight may behold."

Sir Galahad looked upon the glory of the blessed cup, and prayed: "Now, Blessed Lord, would I no longer live." The Quest of the Holy Grail had been fulfilled only by the perfect knight of King Arthur's court.

Most truly has this painter of King Arthur's court and the Quest of his Knights for the Holy Grail, by his skilful hand, his fine imagination, his keen eyes which saw beauty in all things, made them live before our eyes.

THE END

BIBLIOGRAPHY

ANDERSON, A. J.
The Admirable Painter: A Study of Leonardo da Vinci
The Joyous Friar: The Romance of Fra Filippo Lippi

ARMSTRONG, E.
Lorenzo de' Medici and Florence in the Fifteenth Century

BARLOW, T. D.
Albrecht Dürer, His Life and Work

BAXTER, SYLVESTER
The Legend of the Holy Grail as Set Forth in the Frieze by E. A. Abbey

BELL, NANCY R. E.
Representative Painters of the Nineteenth Century

BERENSON, BERNHARD
The Drawings of the Florentine Painters

BOULTON, WILLIAM B.
Thomas Gainsborough

BROWN, GERARD BALDWIN
Rembrandt

BRYANT, LORINDA MUNSON (MRS.)
American Pictures and Their Painters
French Pictures and Their Painters

CAFFIN, CHARLES HENRY
American Painters of the Sea
The Story of American Painting
The Story of Dutch Painting

CALVERT, ALBERT F.
El Greco

COX, KENYON
Winslow Homer
CUNNINGHAM, ALLAN
The Lives of the Most Eminent British Painters and Sculptors—Volume 1
CURTIS AND CAMERON
The Holy Grail: An explanation of the meaning of the series of panels composing E. A. Abbey's frieze decoration in the Boston Public Library
DAVIES, GERALD STANLEY
Frans Hals
DE LA RAMÉE, LOUISE (OUIDA)
The Child of Urbino
DILLON, EDWARD
Rubens
DOWNES, WILLIAM HOWE
Life and Works of Winslow Homer
DÜRER, ALBRECHT
Records of Journeys to Venice and the Low Countries. (Edited by Roger Fry)
DURET, THEODORE
Whistler. (Translated by Frank Rutter)
ELIAS, EDITH L.
In Stuart Times
EVELYN, JOHN
Diary of John Evelyn, F.R.S.
FIELDING, MANTLE
Gilbert Stuart's Portraits of George Washington
FRAPRIE, FRANK ROY
The Raphael Book
FULLER, WILLIAM H.
Gainsborough's Blue Boy

GALLATIN, A. E.
Vermeer of Delft
GRIERSON, ELIZABETH W. (MRS.)
Peeps at Great Cities—Florence
HALE, PHILIP LESLIE
Jan Vermeer of Delft
HARE, CHRISTOPHER
Life and Letters in the Italian Renaissance
HOEBER, ARTHUR
The Barbizon Painters
HOLROYD, SIR CHARLES
Michael Angelo Buonarroti
HORNE, OLIVE BROWNE AND SCOBEY, KATHERINE
Stories of Great Artists
HUMPHREY, GRACE
Women in American History
KNACKFUSS, HERMANN
Van Dyck. (Translated by Campbell Dodgson)
LANIER, SIDNEY
The Boy's King Arthur: Being Sir Thomas Malory's History of King Arthur and his Knights of the Round Table
LAVER, JAMES
Whistler
LUCAS, E. V.
Edwin Austin Abbey
Vermeer of Delft
MACLEOD, MARY
King Arthur and His Noble Knights
MCSPADDEN, JOSEPH WALKER
Famous Painters of America
MATHER, FRANK JEWETT
A History of Italian Painting

MEYNELL, EVERARD
Corot and His Friends
MOORE, T. STURGE
Albrecht Dürer
PEPYS, SAMUEL
Diary written when Pepys was Secretary to the Admiralty in the reigns of Charles II and James II
PERKINS, F. MASON
Giotto
REUMONT, ALFRED VON
Lorenzo de' Medici, The Magnificent
REYNOLDS, VICTOR (Editor)
Stories of the Flemish and Dutch Artists
RICHTER, JEAN PAUL
The Literary Works of Leonardo da Vinci
ROLLAND, ROMAIN
Millet
RUTTER, FRANK
James McNeill Whistler: An Estimate and a Biography
SALTER, E. GURNEY, (Translator)
Bonaventura's Life of Saint Francis
SCOTT, WILLIAM BELL
Albrecht Dürer
SINGER, HANS W.
Stories of the German Artists
SIREN, OSVALD
Leonardo da Vinci
SMITH, CHARLES SPRAGUE
Barbizon Days
STEEDMAN, AMY
Knights of Art

Steele, Robert (Translator)
Little Flowers of Saint Francis
The Mirror of Perfection

Stephens, Frederic George
English Children as Painted by Sir Joshua Reynolds

Streeter, A.
Great Masters in Painting and Sculpture

Strutt, Edward C.
Fra Filippo Lippi

Symonds, John Addington
Michelangelo Buonarroti

Tomson, Arthur
Jean François Millet and the Barbizon School

Vasari, Giorgio
Lives of Seventy of the Most Eminent Painters, Sculptors, and Architects: (Edited by E. H. and E. W. Blashfield and A. A. Hopkins)

Whistler, James Abbott McNeill
The Gentle Art of Making Enemies

Whitcomb, Ida Prentice
Young People's Story of Art

466 493